Praise for *Exodus Cry*

A passionate read! Jim Goll's perspectives are compelling.

CHÉ AHN
SENIOR PASTOR, HARVEST ROCK CHURCH
PASADENA, CALIFORNIA

Exodus Cry is must reading for those who want to understand and
be part of one of the great end-time events in history—the restoration
of Israel and the Jewish people. Jim Goll is a true prophet of God
with a divine message that must be heard and heeded.

JONATHAN BERNIS
DIRECTOR, JEWISH VOICE MINISTRIES INTERNATIONAL

Many people talk about loving the Jewish people. Jim Goll puts feet
to his talk. God's heart and purpose for Israel are very
important subjects for this hour.

MIKE BICKLE
DIRECTOR, INTERNATIONAL HOUSE OF PRAYER
KANSAS CITY, MISSOURI

A simple yet penetrating presentation of God's heart for Israel, this book is a passionate call to turn from the anti-Semitism of the past and present and cooperate with the Holy Spirit in prayer, fasting and practical action. The modern Exodus is upon us, and it's time to line up with God's historic purposes for the nation that brought us the Bible and the Messiah. *Exodus Cry* is written with great prophetic integrity and comes from one who has a proven ministry at the cutting edge of God's purposes in the earth today. Our response to it will determine future history.

COLIN W. DYE
PASTOR, KENSINGTON TEMPLE, LONDON CITY CHURCH
LONDON, ENGLAND

I rejoice over the prayer initiative presented in this book! May God give it wings. Israel gave birth to the Church in the first century; it is the calling of the Church to give birth to Israel in the last.

LARS ENARSON
PRESIDENT, THE WATCHMAN INTERNATIONAL
ISRAEL

Here we see God's heart and intentions for the restoration and redemption of Israel and the Jewish people. Jim Goll issues a clarion call to the Church to participate in God's plan through repentance, intercession and God-directed deeds of righteousness.

DON FINTO
AUTHOR OF *YOUR PEOPLE SHALL BE MY PEOPLE*
NASHVILLE, TENNESSEE

Wisdom is calling out to the Body of Christ to boldly identify with the nation of Israel, the origin of God's promises. *Exodus Cry* will stir you to embrace the place of our spiritual history and ultimate future. Highly recommended!

KINGSLEY A. FLETCHER
SENIOR PASTOR, LIFE COMMUNITY CHURCH
RESEARCH TRIANGLE PARK, NORTH CAROLINA

Jim Goll has indeed written a book for such a time as this. With extensive historical information, deep prophetic insight and the passionate heart of an intercessor, he has sounded the shofar, calling forth a people possessed by G-d. In his plea that we seek the heart of the Father concerning the Jewish people and their destiny, Goll warns us not to forget what G-d remembers and challenges us to love the things that He loves—specifically His covenant people, the Jews. The author quotes the words of the philosopher Santayana, inscribed on a wall at the Auschwitz death camp: "He who does not learn from the lessons of history is doomed to repeat them." No one reading and heading *Exodus Cry* need ever fall into that category.

MARTY GOETZ
MESSIANIC JEWISH RECORDING ARTIST

As the Church we have a mandate from God to bless Israel (see Gen. 12:3). The problem that church leadership faces is how to motivate, instruct and inspire their people to do it. With this book Jim Goll will put the words in our mouths and an urgency in our hearts.

KEN GOTT
METRO CHURCH
TYNE AND WEAR, ENGLAND

There may be no more important ministry assignment to the Church of the new millennium! Superficial good feelings about Israel and excitement over prophetic events are no substitute for ignited, discerning intercession. Leaders and congregations—let us pray!

JACK W. HAYFORD
CHANCELLOR, THE KING'S SEMINARY
VAN NUYS, CALIFORNIA

This is one of the most timely prophetic books I have ever read. If a book like this had been written prior to the Holocaust, history would look a lot different today. Every believer needs to read this book.

CINDY JACOBS
COFOUNDER, GENERALS OF INTERCESSION
COLORADO SPRINGS, COLORADO

Jim Goll presents a challenge to the Church to participate in prayerful intercession and practical support for Israel as God's purposes unfold in these historic times. With inspiring accounts of God's direction and intervention, Goll sounds a clear and passionate call to all believers to understand the times we live in, so that history can be written in the power and anointing of God.

FREDA LINDSAY
COFOUNDER, CHRIST FOR THE NATIONS

Jim Goll shows us how to pray in the events that will signal a release of the Spirit of God in the earthly realm like we have never seen before. His call to the Church is very clear and opens the door for Christians to understand and accept their role in the final destiny of Israel and the Jewish people. May the burden of the Lord rest on you in a new way as you read this book.

Chuck D. Pierce
President, Glory of Zion International
Denton, Texas

If you don't read this book, you could miss the prophetic purpose of God for this last generation. With a keen understanding of the strategic importance of the Jew in God's plan, Jim Goll locates and places missing pieces of the prophetic puzzle. *Exodus Cry* is important reading for this final hour!

Sid Roth
President, Messianic Vision
Brunswick, Georgia

Exodus Cry offers enlightenment to the Church regarding the severe and appalling persecution of Jews by Christians through the ages. Jim Goll calls for heartfelt repentance and intercessory prayer accompanied by active deeds of love. This call is especially urgent at this moment because the door is presently open to Russian Jews, and it may close forever unless God's people respond.

John and Paula Sandford
Cofounders, Elijah House International
Hayden, Idaho

Jim Goll walks us through the miraculous fulfillment of God's promises for a second great Exodus. This is an exciting challenge to believers everywhere to take a radical stand on the side of God's chosen people.

DUTCH SHEETS
AUTHOR OF *INTERCESSORY PRAYER* AND *WATCHMAN PRAYER*
COLORADO SPRINGS, COLORADO

Exodus Cry weaves a tapestry of Jewish history with the biblical prophecy for today. Jim Goll writes with passion, clarity and purpose as he unfolds God's desire for the Church to stand in the gap for the Jewish people. This book stirred and challenged me. Please read this powerful, timely book today!

ALICE SMITH
EXECUTIVE DIRECTOR, U.S. PRAYER CENTER
HOUSTON, TEXAS

Do you want to be close to the heart of God? Then get close to the things that are next to God's heart. Few can blow the trumpet of intercession like Jim Goll. *Exodus Cry* directs you into the purpose of God for Israel and the Jewish people. Read it and act!

TOMMY TENNEY
AUTHOR OF *THE GOD CHASERS* AND *GOD'S DREAM TEAM*
PINEVILLE, LOUISIANA

Exodus Cry is a trumpet call to the Church to arise out of apathy, sounding a prophetic call to intercession for the Jewish people at this strategic moment in time. Jim Goll does a marvelous job of tracing anti-Semitism and the plight of the Jewish people down through the ages. May the history books record the breaking of an anti-Semitic spirit by a Church that demonstrates the life of the Messiah!

BARBARA WENTROBLE
AUTHOR OF *PROPHETIC INTERCESSION* AND *YOU ARE ANOINTED*
DUNCANVILLE, TEXAS

Exodus Cry

JIM W. GOLL

Regal

A Division of Gospel Light
Ventura, California, U.S.A.

Published by Regal Books
A Division of Gospel Light
Ventura, California, U.S.A.
Printed in the U.S.A.

Regal Books is a ministry of Gospel Light, an evangelical Christian publisher dedicated to serving the local church. We believe God's vision for Gospel Light is to provide church leaders with biblical, user-friendly materials that will help them evangelize, disciple and minister to children, youth and families.

It is our prayer that this Regal book will help you discover biblical truth for your own life and help you meet the needs of others. May God richly bless you.

For a free catalog of resources from Regal Books/Gospel Light, please call your Christian supplier or contact us at 1-800-4-GOSPEL *or* www.regalbooks.com.

Cover and Interior Design by Robert Williams
Edited by Larry Walker and Steven Lawson
Interior Photography by David Fitzpatrick

Library of Congress Cataloging-in-Publication Data
Goll, Jim W.
    Exodus cry/Jim W. Goll
       p. cm.
    Includes bibliographical references.
    ISBN 0-8307-2648-9
    1. Judaism (Christian theology)—Miscellanea. 2. Jews—Russia (Federation)—Miscellanea. 3. Private revelations. I. Title.

BT93 .G655 2001
248.2'9—dc21   2001019370

1 2 3 4 5 6 7 8 9 10 11 12 13 14 15 / 09 08 07 06 05 04 03 02 01

Rights for publishing this book in other languages are contracted by Gospel Literature International (GLINT). GLINT also provides technical help for the adaptation, translation and publishing of Bible study resources and books in scores of languages worldwide. For further information, write to GLINT, P.O. Box 4060, Ontario, CA 91761-1003, U.S.A. You may also send e-mail to Glintint@aol.com, or visit the GLINT website at www.glint.org.

DEDICATION

In the hope that "The Cry" will be picked up

by a large portion of the global Body of Christ,

I dedicate this book to the faithful people in the

Worldwide Prayer Movement and to all those

who will join us in interceding for God's

purposes for the Jewish people. It is for you

that this book has been written.

With a love to pray,

JIM W. GOLL

CONTENTS

PART I
Putting the Pieces into Place—
A Historical Perspective

PART II
A Radical and Sudden Change—
A Contemporary Miracle

PART III
A Prophetic Proclamation— Gazing into the Future

FOREWORD

I have just finished rereading Jim Goll's *Exodus Cry* and I am deeply stirred in my spirit. The timing of God is upon our generation.

Many years ago in the land of Midian, an 81-year-old Moses heard the voice of God speaking from a burning bush. God was calling Moses to participate with Him in the fulfillment of a promise spoken centuries earlier to the children of Israel. When the *promise* of God and the *timing* of God intersect, as they did in the days of Moses, we are ripe for an encounter with God and a call to cooperate with Him in the fulfillment of His work.

We are living in another day when promise and timing are intersecting. Amos 3:7 says that God will speak to his prophets when He is preparing to act. Not just to one prophet but to many—a plurality of prophets. God's prophets are speaking today. The timing of God is upon us. He is calling His people to be alert and ready for action.

In the mid '80s, a group of prophetic intercessors began to hear the Lord speaking about the fall of communism and the return of the Russian Jews. Men like Paul Cain, Kjell Sjoberg, Johannes Facius, Steve Lightle, Gustav Scheller and others often traveled great distances to perform prophetic actions that would herald the coming work of God.

In the years since those early prophetic actions, 1 million Russian Jewish people have been released from a 70-year stint of captivity in the former Soviet Union, reminiscent of an earlier 70-year period of captivity before prophets and world leaders of another day united to usher in God's predicted restoration.

The Lord is not finished with restoration. Jim Goll brings together an expansive knowledge of the prophetic with a personal acquaintance with prophetic people. He speaks of dreams and visions that he and his wife, Michal Ann, and others have had regarding a new wave of persecution and an enlarged stream of Russian Jews returning to the Land. Jim is calling the Church to intercession and to action. We have "a chance to rewrite history," he told a group in Hanover, Germany. Yes, God is affording the Church another opportunity to love and bless the Jewish people.

Just as in the days of Esther, the Haman spirit of genocide against the Jewish people is still at work all across the planet. God is looking for Mordecais and Esthers who will protect, shield, harbor and support the Jewish people. Esther risked her life to save her people, but she entered the king's chamber only after three days of prayer and fasting by her uncle Mordecai and his associates. Jim and other prophets are calling for "Esther" to be released, but only after "Mordecai" spends appropriate time in prayer and fasting.

I urge you not to speed-read this book. Read it carefully and prayerfully, and enter into full participation with God in His work in our day.

Dr. Don Finto
The Caleb Company
Nashville, Tennessee

ACKNOWLEDGMENTS

It has not been an easy task to assimilate this project called *Exodus Cry*. The breadth of this work was more than what one person could accomplish. But once again, the Lord assembled an awesome team of servants who believed in the vision and rallied to the cause.

Special thanks goes to my research and development team of Larry Walker, Steven Lawson, Avner Boskey and John Belt, and to my constant consultant, my wife, Michal Ann.

If you have appreciated the photos of art taken primarily in the former Soviet Union and wish to obtain copies or more information, you may contact my friend, photographer David Fitzpatrick, at Pilgrim's Images, P.O. Box 3561, Brentwood, TN 37024-3561.

I also wish to acknowledge my teachers and instructors in the Lord who have helped to pave the expanse of understanding I presently hold on this simple and yet sometimes complex subject. The writings of Derek Prince have had more impact on my life than those of any other person. The pens of Dr. Michael L. Brown, Dr. Dan Juster and others have helped to shape my worldview. The friendship of Avner Boskey, Dr. Don Finto, Jonathan Bernis, Richard Glickstein, David Fitzpatrick and others has been a delight and a source of strength.

Thanks also go to the leadership and the staff of Regal Books for taking the dare with me on this project. And thanks go to our Messiah who stands all day long with His arms outstretched to His obstinate and disobedient children. Thank you, Lord!

INTRODUCTION

This book has been burning in my bones for many years. It does not have a clear end. Rather, it is an invitation to take a journey, to participate in making history. It is a call to prayer before the throne of almighty God and a daring challenge to be an answer to those prayers.

Exodus Cry is an exhortation to Gentile Christians to receive God's heart for the Jewish people. For Jewish people, both those who have accepted Christ as their Messiah and those who have yet to consider Him, this is a wake-up call to the times we are about to face.

Written with multiple sets of lenses, this manuscript weaves together

- an appreciation of history
- an overview of the unique relationship between the Church and Israel
- the interplay of the prophetic and prayer
- a call to action

This book also acts as a visual guide. I have included photos of some of the sites where my friends and I have lived and visited as we traversed the lands of the former Soviet Union, the Middle East and beyond.

Written from a prophetic and historical perspective, this journal traces God's footprints as He has been faithful to fulfill His promises to the people of Israel. As you walk along this trail with me, you will catch a glimpse of God's willingness to go to any length to see His Word become reality!

While ministering in England in 1999, my wife, Michal Ann, was given a dream that has become a guiding light. It supplied the spark and the vision for this book. In this vivid dream, Michal Ann was shown a puzzle of the sky. It was called The Horizon of Time. The interlocking pieces were mixed up, waiting to be properly assembled. As she peered at the sky, she had a strong sense of the lifelong call of God that rested upon our lives to help put together the pieces of a puzzle that would show God's purposes among the Jewish people. The puzzle in Michal Ann's vision included pieces from the past, the present and the future. I have followed the same basic outline in this book.

Part one, titled "Putting the Pieces into Place—A Historical Perspective," sets the framework. We look back at the first Great Exodus and begin to understand God's purposes. The second part, "A Radical and Sudden Change—A Contemporary Miracle," describes the dramatic events that occurred in late 1980s and throughout the 1990s, events that literally reshaped the face of the world. The third part of this moving drama is called "A Prophetic Proclamation—Gazing into the Future." In this section, we take out our telescope and set our sight on the horizon. We focus on God's yet-to-be-revealed purposes. We ponder how He will put together the final pieces of the puzzle.

At the back of this book, I have included a wealth of resources. The appendices include overviews of both Israeli and Russian history, the dates of Purim, a list of prayer points, a reference list of ministries active in putting the pieces of the puzzle together, a recommended reading list and a glossary of terms.

Why read *Exodus Cry*? Because it will stir you to step forward to do exploits for Jesus Christ! You will be touched by the fire of

God and prompted to take your place as an intercessor. You will long to be at the core of His prophetic promises and appointments. You will be ready to take a stand, to release intervention and to cut off the enemy's plans through the power of crisis intercession.

Come walk in the shoes of many pioneers of the faith. It is a new season. Grab hold of the prophetic baton and lift your voice on behalf of God's chosen ones, the people of Israel. Together we can see the completion of the Great Second Exodus, which has already begun to unfold before our eyes!

PART I

PUTTING THE PIECES INTO PLACE

A HISTORICAL PERSPECTIVE

CHAPTER 1

THE COMING-OUT PARTY

I will say to the north, "Give them up!" And to the south, "Do not hold them back." Bring My sons from afar and My daughters from the ends of the earth.

ISAIAH 43:6

"In 18 months 'the hunters' will begin to be released to hunt down the Russian Jews." The audible voice[1] of the Lord awakened me with these words early Easter Sunday morning in April 1999. The bedroom in our home, then located in Hunter's Run in Antioch, Tennessee, was filled with the presence of the fear of God. The Lord had my full attention: I trembled as I tried to comprehend His sobering words.

More understanding came as riveting waves of the destiny of God rolled over me. Quietly, the Holy Spirit began to speak. The Lord said that our family would move from our urban residence in Hunter's Run to a place of seclusion. The relocation, of course, would affect our family, but it was also a prophetic statement. God was calling for His people to draw closer to Him, to make Him their secret hiding place.

Being thrust forth from Hunter's Run in the flesh would serve as a barometer in the Spirit, giving a reading of future events concerning the Jewish people. This Easter morning message was a wake-up call to pray—*a call to crisis intervention.*

Six weeks later, my wife, Michal Ann, and I ministered at Ken and Lois Gott's Revival Now! Spring Conference in Sunderland,

England, along with Cindy Jacobs, Brenda Kilpatrick and others. The fires of renewal have burned brightly in Sunderland for some time, and the people at the gathering were hungry for more of God. Along with Michal Ann and our family, we had brought with us a group of 30 intercessors crying out for "more, Lord!"

When Cindy Jacobs took the microphone to pray over a couple of people, the power of the Holy Spirit seemed to overtake her. Cindy is recognized internationally for her authority and accuracy in intercession and prophecy. While prophetically declaring God's purposes for Lois Gott and northern England, to my amazement she uttered, "There is coming an exodus of Jews from across Russia—and they will come across the North Sea seeking refuge."

Unbeknown to Cindy, about 18 months earlier Lois Gott had learned that her grandfather was Jewish. Later in the meeting, Cindy added that doors of escape from the "Land of the North" could begin to close and that increased anti-Semitism would start to produce an exodus of Jewish people from that region. The crowd was electrified with an overwhelming sense of the destiny of God. The jealousy of God was present and everyone knew it.

A quick mental calculation confirmed that Cindy's prophetic word matched the message and the timing contained in the prophetic declaration I had received on Easter. Both warnings carried an immediate urgency, although the two of us had never talked with each other about these issues. *Yes, God does confirm His word, and it seemed that was exactly what transpired in England on that eventful afternoon!*

THE CHURCH MUST
RESPOND NOW!

Six months later, when members of the World Prayer Movement gathered for the World Congress on Intercession in Colorado

Springs, Colorado, a third witness was added to this word. On December 4, which happened to be the first day of the Jewish Feast of Dedication (Hanukkah), the burden of the Lord exploded like a volcanic eruption. Dr. C. Peter Wagner, a respected theologian, missiologist and international prayer leader, read a statement prepared by the Apostolic Council of Prophetic Elders, a group of nationally recognized and gifted prophetic men and women who had met privately for two days prior to the prayer convocation. Wagner warned that anti-Semitism in Russia would soon escalate to the point where "it requires *an immediate response from the Church in prayer* [to] help open a window of escape for those who feel called to leave and protection to those who are called to stay."[2]

As Wagner read these words, a sense of urgency swept through the audience. It seemed God was about to stage a replay of the Great Exodus described in the Old Testament. Strong intercession arose as we cried out for the Lord's purposes to be fulfilled with the Jewish people in the former Soviet Union and around the world.

How could this sense of urgency be communicated to the Church? How could we make known the understanding that prayer can both unlock prophetic promises and be a tool to cut off, shorten or delay revelations of judgment? How could we join together and impart to others these two great ministries of prayer and the prophetic? How could we awaken the global Body of Christ to God's purposes for the Church and Israel?

It took God's intervention for the first exodus of Jewish people to occur, when Moses led his people out of captivity. Would it take anything less for the completion of a second Great Exodus?

The Miracle of the First Exodus

Nothing in human history compares to the miracle of the Great Exodus of the Jewish people from Egyptian slavery to the Promised

Statue in Kishnev, Moldavia

Land. Yet the Old Testament episode suffers from what I call the storybook syndrome. When, over a long period of time, from generation to generation, we retell a true event, we tend to trade the power of its miraculous reality for its storybook charm. Any possibility that such miracles could or would take place today becomes laughable—those who dare to believe in a miracle-working God become the butt of the joke.

There are major problems with the human habit of minimizing the miraculous: The events described in the book of Exodus *actually happened* and *God still works miracles*. It is equally unwise to downgrade God's current relationship with the Jewish people. He *still loves the Jewish people* and *He is not done with them.* In the book of Jeremiah, God said:

> "Therefore behold, the days are coming," declares the LORD, "when they will no longer say, 'As the LORD lives, who brought up the sons of Israel *from the land of Egypt,*' but, 'As the LORD lives, who brought up and led back the descendants of the household of Israel *from* the *north land* and *from all the countries where I had driven them.*' Then they will live on their own soil" (Jer. 23:7,8, emphasis mine).

AN EYEWITNESS ACCOUNT

Before we look at a second exodus, let's go back to the Great Exodus—the one Moses led—this time with a fictionalized retelling by someone who was there. For this eyewitness report we turn to Hoshea ben Nun,[3] also known as Joshua:

The piercing scream awoke everyone in the dirt-floored house. I scrambled to my feet and was the first to peer through the doorway into the inky darkness of the Egyptian night. A sudden shiver raced through my body.

Something of incomprehensible power and size passed over my father's humble home. It was not the night chill that made me shake; I had slept fully dressed for the first time in my life and was ready for flight, just as the prophet Moses had instructed us seven days earlier.

This was the 10th judgment of Jehovah to strike the land of pharaoh. With it came a mysterious brooding force that seemed to fill the air. As if upon a signal, blood-curdling screams and sorrowful wails shot across the great capital city of Rameses and throughout the chambers of Pi-Ramesse, the royal residence of pharaoh.[4] Moses had warned every Hebrew family not to venture from home until sunrise. Even though I could not step outside, I knew that some of the terrifying sounds came from the homes of my Egyptian neighbors. Once more, the prophet's prediction had come true.

Moses had assembled our entire congregation. His instructions were clear. He warned every Jewish household to choose a one-year-old male lamb and to eat unleavened bread. Seven days later, we began what has since become known as Passover. At twilight every Hebrew household, including mine, sacrificed its lamb and sprinkled blood upon the lintels and doorposts of their house, adding a handful of hyssop. We knew God was up to something.

My name is Hoshea, but you can call me Joshua. I will never forget the way I felt as I watched my father, Nun, meticulously following Moses' commands. I had helped him burn the remains and unbroken bones of the lamb immediately after the hastily prepared meal. Although I was a just a young man, I knew this was an important event that would change the way we lived forever. But it was not the first inexplicable event to occur since Moses and his brother Aaron had reappeared on the scene, returning from the wilderness the Egyptians call the Red Lands.

At first they performed signs and wonders that dazzled the Jewish elders. Then Moses confronted pharaoh with a command from the God of the Hebrews: "Let My people go!"

Pharaoh refused to release our people, even after Aaron's rod consumed the rods of Egypt's greatest sorcerers, Jannes and Jambres.[5]

In response, the Holy One, our God, told Moses to confront pharaoh the next morning, when he went out to the water to awaken Amun-Re, the Egyptian sun god.[6]

When pharaoh came to the water in the morning with his servants and sorcerer-counselors, Moses and Aaron met them. They reminded Egypt's ruler of God's command. As God had instructed, Aaron dipped his staff in the waters of the Nile. The river instantly turned to blood! Even the water in small streams, ponds, stone pitchers and wooden buckets turned crimson. The very lifeline that made Egypt great while surrounded by deserts was instantly polluted. God had profaned and humbled Aman-Re.[7]

Under pharaoh's glare, the magicians of Egypt also tried to turn water to blood, but it was a trick. No one could reverse the judgment of Jehovah or remove the stench of the dying fish along the Nile. Even my family and all of the Hebrews had to dig for untainted water in the silt-rich banks of the Nile. Despite widespread fear, the magicians' sorcery seemed to be enough to once again turn pharaoh's heart to stone.

Seven days later, God sent Moses and Aaron to challenge pharaoh again. When Egypt's ruler refused to let our Hebrew people go, Moses told Aaron to stretch out his staff over the waters of Egypt. Instantly, from the already polluted waters of the Nile, a swarm of frogs emerged to invade pharaoh's entire kingdom (including my father's home). Many of pharaoh's people worshiped frogs as household deities, but on that day, their "gods" became tools in the hand of the One True God to punish the captors of the Hebrew people.[8]

Jannes and Jambres managed to conjure some frogs out of the Nile, but pharaoh doubted their ability to match the power of the God of the Hebrews. He promised Moses he would let the Hebrew people go if the plague of frogs was removed. The following day Moses prayed to God, and all of the frogs died (except those that remained in their natural habitat). But the stench from the mounds of decaying frog remains blanketed mighty Egypt, causing pharaoh to again harden his heart, and he reneged on his promise.

Moses told Aaron to strike the dust of the earth with his staff. When Aaron obeyed, God released the third plague, miraculously transforming tiny grains of desert dust into biting, stinging, clinging gnats or lice. Pharaoh's magicians could not duplicate this creative miracle on any scale. They reluctantly declared it to be "the finger of God." Pharoah, however, refused to listen. Meanwhile, in the Valley of the Kings in Thebes, the sands came alive with hordes of gnats. There were so many that they dimmed the brilliant splendor of the Shrine of Ptah in Memphis. The gnats even invaded my people's humble dwellings in Goshen, as well as the major cities of Egypt.[9]

That was the last plague to touch the Hebrews under pharaoh's rule, for the Holy One had warned the Egyptian ruler through Moses that He would set apart His people. However, one after another, the judgments of God continued to rain down upon the Egyptians.

The fourth terror of Jehovah—swarms of insects that invaded and covered every house, temple and person, and laid waste to every field in Egypt—brought pharaoh to repentance, but only in part.[10]

Pharaoh agreed to allow Moses to offer sacrifices to God, but only *within* Egypt's borders. That was not good enough. God released a fifth plague that struck at the heart of two of Egypt's three chief demon gods.

As Moses promised to pharaoh, the day after their meeting, a fatal livestock disease struck down every bull, calf, horse, donkey, camel and hoofed animal in Egypt.

It was a slap in the face of pharaoh and Egypt's powerful priests, Amon and Ptah, the bull god. There was nothing the Egyptians could do to prevent it. The disease did not strike any Hebrew herds, flocks or stalls. All the Hebrews in Egypt *knew* that God was protecting us.[11] This infuriated and frightened the Egyptian leaders and caused pharaoh's heart to grow even harder toward Jehovah.

The boils came next. At God's command, Moses took a handful of soot from one of the countless brick kilns where many Hebrews labored each day. With the soot in his hand, he confronted pharaoh. He threw the soot toward the sky and instantly every Egyptian and every one of their animals that had survived the livestock disease was covered with painful, burning boils or pus-filled sores. The boils hit pharaoh's magicians so hard that they could not stand up to look Moses in the face. Yet none of the Hebrew people or their animals was touched.[12] As God predicted, pharaoh's heart only grew harder.

The seventh judgment was more frightening than any of the others. Jehovah warned pharaoh that He would strike Egypt with a killing hail, but graciously

God warned pharaoh to shelter his people and all the animals that were still alive. A few wise Egyptians sought cover, but many did not.[13]

When Moses stretched his hand and rod toward the sky, thunder, hail and fire fell from the heavens, killing everything and everyone that was not under a roof or shelter. Two of Egypt's four main crops were instantly destroyed.[14] Amazingly, the Hebrews were not harmed. Pharaoh pleaded with Moses to pray that the hail would stop. The prophet complied, but waited until the next day, once he was outside the royal city.

To pharaoh's relief, the hail ceased. Feeling a renewed sense of security, he again changed his mind and refused to let the people of Israel leave. But pharaoh was about to learn that God had *not* changed His mind.

After Moses warned the king of Egypt to let the Hebrew people go or prepare for an eighth judgment, pharaoh's counselors begged him to keep his word. But he only gave permission for the Hebrew men to go. That was not good enough for Moses, or for God.

The following day a great army of locusts descended on Egypt from the east and consumed every trace of the wheat and spelt harvests, the two remaining food crops of the land. The flying pests destroyed every tree and even invaded the houses and barns. It was a shocking sight: locusts piled high in the fields and on the streets.

The priests of the cult of Osiris, the Egyptian god of the dead, could not continue their annual mystery rituals because of the locust swarm, and all mummification operations were brought to a halt in Abydos.[15] As bad as the locusts were, what followed was even worse.

As usual, pharaoh quickly repented and asked Moses to pray that the locusts would be removed. As soon as

Moses interceded, the locusts were driven into the Red Sea. But again Egypt's leader broke his word and refused to let the Hebrew people leave.

God responded with a commandment. He told Moses to stretch his hand toward the sky. When Moses obeyed, a thick darkness descended over the land of Egypt. The Egyptians who experienced it told me they could actually *feel* the darkness, as if it settled over their souls as well as over the land!

No candle, torch or oil lamp could penetrate the darkness or even provide enough light to see in houses! For three full days, none of the Egyptians even moved beyond the doors of their homes.[16]

No one was more terrified than the powerful priests of Re, the sun god. Gloomy darkness blanketed Re's temple at Heiropolis (the city of the sun). The priests attempted every ritual, including sacrifices, but no effort could keep them from being openly humbled by the God of the Hebrews. The mighty Re and his servants were helpless before Jehovah for three days. Yet every Hebrew home in the land of pharaoh had light. *The chains of bondage began to drop away in the light of Jehovah's glory.*

Pharaoh finally gave in. One day, he told Moses to take the Hebrew people and leave—without their flocks and herds. When Moses told him they needed their animals, pharaoh threatened to kill the prophet of God if there was another affliction upon the Egyptians. That was when God released the 10th plague, the death of every firstborn person in Egypt and of the cattle as well.

One agonized scream after another blended together to pierce the night in a heartbreaking litany of sorrow, abruptly interrupting my thoughts. *It won't be long now*, I thought.

That night, pharaoh urged Moses to take every Hebrew and their flocks and leave Egypt immediately. All of the Egyptians were saying, "Leave quickly or we will *all* be dead!"[17]

We were all packed and ready when the word came. On the way to the gathering point, we each asked our Egyptian neighbors for valuable jewelry, an action Moses had commanded. The Egyptians willingly showered us with gold and silver, which were later used to make the instruments and furniture of the Tabernacle of God.

Six hundred thousand Hebrew men and their families were the first to go. Each man carried weapons, also gathered from the Egyptians.[18] One day we were a slave people, the next we left as the army of Jehovah.

No one attempted to bar the way or protest the exodus. In fact, the dogs did not even bark as we filed through the royal city of Rameses on the way to freedom.[19]

An estimated 3 million people followed Moses from Rameses' gates to Succoth. God provided a tower of clouds to lead us by day and a pillar of fire to warm us at night.

The 24-mile journey that first day was a challenge, but it also took some time to become familiar with sleeping in the glare of the pillar of fire.

At first light, on the second day, we began an even longer, 38-mile journey to Etham, on the edge of the desert. The following morning the tower of clouds led us in a different direction, to a place bordered by a wall of towering rocks, impossibly deep gorges and the sea.[20]

Moses later told us that God purposely "leaked" our location to pharaoh and hardened the hearts of pharaoh and his advisors. Pharaoh had decided it was a mistake to release his "free labor force." He gathered his state-of-the-art armored chariot divisions, including his hand-chosen team of 600 elite charioteers, and began a hot pursuit. He had no idea that the God of the Hebrews was leading his army to destruction.

Just as pharaoh's army spotted the pillar of cloud and he began to anticipate recapturing his escaped slaves, the Hebrews saw the approaching cloud of desert dust and the advancing columns of pharaoh's thousands of horse-drawn chariots of war. Many Hebrews (those with very short memories) felt sure we were destined for destruction and murmured against Moses. But the prophet had an answer:

> Do not fear! Stand by and see the salvation of the LORD which He will accomplish for you today; for the Egyptians whom you have seen today, you will never see them again forever. The LORD will fight for you while you keep silent (Exod. 14:13,14).

Then Moses told the Hebrews to "go forward." They began to walk directly toward the churning waves of the sea as Moses lifted up his staff and stretched out his hand.

My family was in the front section. We watched as a strong wind from the east divided the sea and made a broad path of *dry land* to the other side! The walls of water reared up above our heads so high that we could barely see the top as we walked downward from the seashore toward the far side. We moved forward as a group, with hundreds of people walking side by side on dry ground, interspersed with our herds, flocks and wheeled carts.

Glancing back over my shoulder, I looked into the east wind just before we left the shore. It was at that moment that I saw a bright being standing behind us, alongside the great pillar of cloud, separating us from pharaoh's advancing chariots. The cloud was so brilliant that it lit our way across the sea passage, but everything behind it looked dark. As we took each step forward, I knew we would be safe. God was fighting for us, and no one would get past the cloud of His presence.

As the crossing continued far into the night, the stationary cloud and fearsome angelic being held pharaoh's troops at bay. When the last families and herds reached the halfway point across the Red Sea, Jehovah moved the fiery cloud forward. When the cloud moved, pharaoh's eager forces could barely see the escaping figures of the Hebrews. Not wanting to lose their prey, pharaoh's forces chased the Hebrews into the dry bed of the sea.

We watched in amazement as the last Hebrews reached the far side of the sea, followed by the pillar of cloud and light. Pharaoh's men were clearly visible in the middle of the dry sea passage and they appeared to be making rapid progress toward us.

Suddenly the Egyptian army came to a halt. For no apparent reason, wheels flew off their chariots. Entire ranks of chariots veered into one another and into lines of horsemen on either side. Confusion seized pharaoh's legendary horsemen and charioteers. The last Hebrews to cross onto dry land told us that they heard the Egyptians shouting in the distance, "Let us flee from Israel, for the LORD is fighting for them against the Egyptians."[21]

Then Moses stretched his hand over the sea once more, just as the sun rose in the east. The strong east wind instantly vanished and the standing walls of foaming water suddenly closed in upon pharaoh's army and obliterated them! Mighty Jehovah delivered the Hebrew people from pharaoh's army, and the only proof that they ever existed was the Egyptian bodies that later washed ashore.

Moses led all 3 million Hebrews in songs of joy, triumph and praise to Jehovah. Then his sister, Miriam, took up a tambourine and led a final song of joy for the "coming-out party," marking the end of the Hebrews' 430-year stay under the shadow of the pharaohs.

HAVE WE FORGOTTEN WHAT GOD REMEMBERS?

Twenty-first century man has forgotten what *God remembers*: God made an ancient promise to the Jewish people that He intends to keep.

"Therefore behold, the days are coming," declares the LORD, "when they will no longer say, 'As the LORD lives, who brought up the sons of Israel *from the land of Egypt,*' but, 'As the LORD lives, who brought up and led back the descendants of the household of Israel *from* the *north land* and *from all the countries where I had driven them.*' Then they will live on their own soil" (Jer. 23:7,8, emphasis mine).

Many well-meaning Christians have concluded that the Jewish people and the modern state of Israel play no role in the fulfillment of Bible prophecy, while others set their end-time prophecy clocks by what happens in Israel. Many of these opinions are based upon how the Jewish people themselves view, and react to Jesus the Messiah. It is true that no one can be saved apart from repentance and faith in Him, but we quickly forget that each of us was lost before the Lord pursued and found us in His mercy.

Act upon God's Faithfulness

God's dealings with the children of Israel involve *His faithfulness* more than *their faithfulness*. We should carefully examine God's promises and predictions concerning the Jewish people on the basis of *who made those promises*, not on whether or not the recipients of the promises deserve them.

No one deserves the mercy and grace of God, but He extends them to all of us anyway. God keeps His promises to the thousandth generation (see Deut. 7:9; Ps. 105:8), and He made some promises about the Jewish people that have yet to come to pass. As you will soon see, we are right in the middle of it all!

We now live in a hinge period of time. At the moment, a door of destiny is open for Russian Jews. That door may soon close forever unless God's people pray.

God's Word speaks of *two* great regatherings of the Jewish people from dispersion back to Israel. One took place in Moses' day and is described in the book of Exodus. The other must happen *after* the arrival of the Messiah and before His return:

> "Therefore behold, days are coming," declares the LORD, "when it will no longer be said, 'As the LORD lives, who brought up the sons of Israel *out of the land of Egypt*,' but, 'As the LORD lives, who brought up the sons of Israel *from the land of the north* and *from all the countries* where He had banished them.' For *I will restore them to their own land* which I gave to their fathers" (Jer. 16:14-15, emphasis mine).

God has delivered or restored small remnants of Jewish people from places of captivity to Jerusalem for specific purposes. We see this in the life and ministry of Nehemiah, the prophet, when God opened the way for a remnant to return from Babylonian captivity to rebuild the walls of Jerusalem. Yet none of these restorations meets the criteria for the great ingathering of Jewish people from the Land of the North.

Author and Bible teacher Derek Prince defined "the Land of the North" in his book, *The Last Word on the Middle East*:

> Yet a day is coming, declares Jeremiah, when this great Passover deliverance will pale into insignificance by comparison with the second ingathering of the Jewish people from all lands—particularly from the land of the north, which includes Germany, Poland and Russia.[22]

It takes only a glance at a map to confirm that Eastern Europe is part of the Land of the North. Moscow, the capital of Russia and the former seat of Communism, lies 1660 miles north and just two degrees longitude east of Jerusalem.

The Coming Exodus Will Be the Largest

I believe this last-day ingathering and Second Great Exodus of Jewish people from the Land of the North will eclipse the first Great Exodus from Egypt in magnitude and scope—there will be even greater miraculous signs and wonders. More than 1 million Jewish people have immigrated to Israel from the Land of the North since the reestablishment of the nation of Israel nearly 60 years ago. However, as of this writing, only about one-third of the Jewish people living in the northern regions of the world have made *aliyah* (literally, "going up") to their ancient homeland in Israel. Meanwhile, the door of opportunity in the republics of the former Soviet Union is beginning to close.

God's people have a biblical and moral responsibility to pray. We must act upon His will for the descendants of Abraham, Isaac and Jacob. In the process of this deed of love, many Jewish people will come to know and receive Jesus Christ as the Messiah of promise.

The Lord always uses the hearts and hands of man to accomplish His will in the earth. God spelled out in advance *what* He will do and *how* He will accomplish it. The passage is found in the second part of Jeremiah's prophecy about the Jewish remnant:

> "Behold, I am going to send for *many fishermen*," declares the LORD, "and they will fish for them; and afterwards I will send for *many hunters*, and they will hunt them from every mountain and every hill and from the clefts of the rocks" (Jer. 16:16, bold emphasis mine).

Fishers Lure, Hunters Drive

Some people who are otherwise well versed in the Bible raise their eyebrows in surprise when the subject of "fishers and hunters" comes up. What is Jeremiah talking about? Fishermen use bait to lure and entice something to a desired place. Hunters drive and chase down their quarry, and the ultimate goal is destruction.

God extends mercy before He releases judgment. He has called the descendants of Abraham, Isaac and Jacob to return to their home. First He sends benevolent fishermen to the Jewish people living in the Land of the North to encourage, woo and entice them to obey God's call for all of the benefits they will receive. The fishers are benevolent because they wish only good upon the Jewish people. Their mission is to extend mercy and deliverance *to* a divine destiny and *from* impending danger.

What about the hunters? We will cover this in greater detail in the following chapters, but the Jewish people in Europe received advanced warning about Hitler and his Nazi party from many fishers. Only a few heeded the warning. The day came in 1938 when Hitler released his Gestapo and SS hunters to hunt down and round up every Jewish person they could find. Their goal was the absolute annihilation of the Jewish people. Hitler, among others who hate the Jewish people, followed in a long, historic line of hunters that the Bible warned would come on the scene.

The Second Great Exodus

Today, many prophetic prayer leaders around the globe sense a common thread of urgency concerning the Jewish people and the imminent release of new hunters in the Land of the North. It seems the time has come for a second Great Exodus. In fact, as we will see in later chapters, it is actually already under way.

I am convinced that God intends to release the Jewish people from "the north land and from all the countries where I had driven them" (Jer. 23:8). The primary focus of God's most recent message through prophetic and intercessory prayer leaders is the Jewish people who live in the biblical Land of the North (the area comprised by the former Soviet Union).

As Christians, what is our role in this? I believe that a *revolution* will come to the Church in this decade, the first of the new millennium. A crucial component of this revolution involves a remnant of the Church that *will capture the Father's passion for the Jewish people*, His ancient covenant people. I believe God will breathe life upon this ancient prophecy of Zechariah:

> I will pour out *on the house of David* and on *the inhabitants of Jerusalem,* the Spirit of grace and of supplication, so that they will look on Me whom they have pierced; and they will mourn for Him, as one mourns for an only son, and they will weep bitterly over Him like the bitter weeping over a firstborn (Zech. 12:10, emphasis mine).

I realize there are at least two theological interpretations of this passage, but in my view, this prophetic promise speaks to both the Church and to Israel in a parallel understanding. Jesus is *the* Son of David, and the Church makes up *in part* "the house of David" (see Acts 15:15-17). Gentile followers of Christ are "of the house and lineage of David" because they have been grafted into the Vine, Jesus Christ.

Many Christian leaders stop here, but in the Bible the prophet goes on to say, "*and the inhabitants of Jerusalem.*" We could make a serious mistake by ignoring the *literal* meaning and application of this prophetic passage.

When God is *fervent* about specific people, we cannot afford to be *indifferent* to them. We must not ignore the poor, the downtrodden, the outcast and the lost. And we must not forget His ancient people of old, the Jewish people.

Never Again!

Previous generations of Christians, for the most part, practiced indifference; and by default, spurred on Hitler's evil hatred and persecution of the Jewish people. The failure of the Church to act on biblical principles helped produce the disastrous and tragic consequences of the Holocaust during World War II. Never again!

We must lay aside every preconceived idea, presumption and preference. We need to discover afresh what *God says* He will do with the Jewish people and what role we must play. The future of the world may literally hang in the balance.

CHAPTER 2

THE BIRTH OF A NATION

Who has heard such a thing? Who has seen such things? Can a land be born in one day? Can a nation be brought forth all at once? As soon as Zion travailed, she also brought forth her sons.

ISAIAH 66:8

The well-being of the Jewish people has always hinged on the balance among the level of their obedience to God, His faithful promises to their forefathers and His eternal purpose and love for them. In general terms, just like with the Church, when Jewish people obey Him, they prosper. When they do not, judgment falls upon them.

This principle comes from Deuteronomy 28 and has been repeatedly seen in action in the history of Israel (read Judges 2:6-23!). This biblical law of "sowing and reaping" still applies, even under the grace of God received through the finished work of Jesus Christ.

THE JEWISH HISTORY OF SUFFERING

Over the millennia, Jacob's descendants have suffered greatly and have been greatly blessed as well. British Bible teacher Lance Lambert says of them:

No other nation in the history of mankind has twice been uprooted from its land, scattered to the ends of the earth and then brought back again to that same territory. If the first exile and restoration was remarkable, the second is miraculous. Israel has twice lost its statehood and its national sovereignty, twice had its capital and hub of religious life destroyed, its towns and cities razed to the ground, its people deported and dispersed, and then twice had it all restored again.

Furthermore, no other nation or ethnic group has been scattered to the four corners of the earth, and yet survived as an easily identifiable and recognizable group.[1]

The first exile took place under Babylonian rule. As for the second great exile, Roman forces serving under the Roman commander, Titus, destroyed and dismantled Jerusalem in August A.D. 70, exactly as Jesus prophesied 37 years earlier. The Romans killed 600,000 Jewish residents and deported 300,000 more to locations scattered around the Empire.[2]

Sixty-five years later, Roman Emperor Hadrian's forces crushed the last Jewish uprising which was led by Bar-Cochba. Those forces hated and persecuted Jewish and Gentile followers of Christ. Some observers believe this might have helped plant early seeds of anti-Semitism in the fledgling Church.

Jerusalem Declared "Off Limits"

Hadrian's hatred for the Jews burned so bright that he changed Jerusalem's name to *Aelia Capitolina* (his given name was Aelius) and declared it "a Roman city forever *which no Jew could enter under pain of death.*" He built a temple to Jupiter on the site of the former temple where sacrifices had been made to Jehovah.[3] Then he renamed the land *Syria Palaestina* (Latin for Philistia). Caesar overlooked one "minor" detail: Unlike the powerless gods of Rome, the God of Israel was and is alive and well.

The Jewish people in Jerusalem and Judea were recaptured, died violent deaths or were scattered to distant lands. This second dispersion following the death and resurrection of Jesus the Messiah lasted far longer than the first. It would not end after 500 years, or even 1,000 years.

The devastated city of Jerusalem became the most contested urban real estate on Earth as, for 2,000 years, various nations, empires and religious factions battled for its possession. All the while, its builders and original residents, the Jewish people, were forced to seek refuge in Gentile cities and nations around the world, but could call none of them "home." That all changed in *one day*.

Eighteen hundred seventy-eight years after the destruction of Jerusalem under Titus, a new nation emerged from the birth pangs of Word War II and the horrible Holocaust, as Isaiah prophesied (see the Scripture passage quoted at the beginning of this chapter).

God Sent the "Fishers"

Before every birth there must come birth pangs. The Scriptures clearly predicted the two great dispersions and the persecutions they represented. They also describe the regathering of the Jewish people and the rebirth of Israel. Yet, through world events and the prophetic voices of Christian and Jewish "fishermen," God also warned His people about an impending danger. These divine messengers never used force; they warned and wooed the Jewish people of impending danger and God's plan to deliver those who took heed. In virtually every case, His goal was to preserve a remnant and eventually return them to their ancient Land of Promise.

In 1855, Hudson Taylor, a Christian physician and missionary to China, saw in the Spirit that a great end-time revival would occur in the Land of the North. Taylor was full of the Holy Ghost and entirely surrendered to God. Known as a man of great self-denial, heartfelt compassion and powerful prayer, he interceded for the salvation of the Chinese every morning for 40 years.

Taylor Foresaw a Spiritual Awakening

While on a ministry furlough in England, Taylor suddenly stopped in the middle of a sermon and, for a few moments, stood speechless, with his eyes closed. Finally he explained to his audience:

> I have seen a vision. I saw in this vision a great war that will encompass the whole world. I saw this war recess and then start again, actually being two wars. After this, I saw much unrest and revolts that will affect many nations. I saw in some places, spiritual awakenings. In Russia, I saw there will come a general, all-encompassing, national, spiritual awakening, so great that there could never be another like it. From Russia, I saw the awakening spread to many European countries and then I saw an all-out awakening followed by the coming of Christ.[4]

Twenty-six years later, in 1881, Russia's tsar, Alexander II, was murdered and his son, Alexander III, succeeded him. Alexander III hated the Jewish people, and that year a "pogrom" (an organized massacre or persecution of Jewish people) swept through Kishinev, the capital of Moldova, adjacent to Romania and Ukraine.

As life for the persecuted Jews became more difficult under the tsar, Zionist ideas about a Jewish homeland gained strength and followers. Some Jewish leaders began to search for a place of refuge, a homeland for the world's displaced Jewish population. The first *aliyah* or immigration to Israel took place in 1882. Jewish immigrants established a Jewish colony called Rishon Lezion. The term "anti-Semitism," entered the English language in 1882 as well, defined as "hostility toward or discrimination against Jews as a religious, ethnic or racial group."[5]

A Dream Is Born

Also in 1882, Joseph Rabinowitz, a prominent Jewish leader, journeyed from Kishinev to Palestine. He was an unofficial delegate representing some like-minded Jews who wanted to see if Palestine (as it was called at that time) was the right place to establish a Jewish homeland.

Rabinowitz was a Haskala or Enlightment Jew who first searched for truth while studying the Talmud with a Chassidic rabbi and later sought understanding through extensive reading of more liberal writings by so-called enlightened Jewish teachers. He deeply loved his people, but disappointments he experienced and witnessed finally convinced him they would find safety among Gentile nations only as long as it was convenient for their unwilling hosts.

During his brief stay in Palestine, Rabinowitz went to the Wailing Wall in Jerusalem at the beginning of a Sabbath day. He watched in dismay as Jews who had gathered there for prayer struggled to worship and weep at the wall amid "the jibes and harassments of the Muslims."[6] (The Sultan of Turkey controlled Palestine at that time from his capital in Constantinople.) The level of desolation Rabinowitz witnessed in the Promised Land shocked him.

What he saw in Palestine, coupled with the situation of the Jewish people in Europe and around the world greatly troubled him. Just before sunset one evening, Rabinowitz visited the Mount of Olives. He sat down on a slope near Gethsemane.

As he pondered the troubling scene, a passage from the Hebrew New Testament he had read 15 years earlier flashed in his mind: "So if the Son makes you free, you will be free indeed" (John 8:36). In that moment, he began to realize that Jesus was the King and Messiah, the only one who could save Israel. Rabinowitz returned to his temporary residence, where he read John's Gospel. He was struck by the passage in John 15:5, "Apart from Me you can do nothing."[7]

Rabinowitz Starts First Messianic Congregation

When Rabinowitz returned home, he studied the Hebrew New Testament. He later played a key role in distributing Bibles to other Jewish people. In Kishinev, he told his Jewish friends about his Mount of Olives experience. He did not claim to know if the land of Palestine was the hope of the Jewish people. Then, touching his chest, he would say, "This is the land, the land of the heart. It is what God wants us to obtain." He would sometimes add, "The key to the Holy Land lies in the hands of our brother, Jesus."[8]

In Kishinev, Rabinowitz and 40 families established the world's first modern-day Hebrew-Christian, or Messianic, congregation, Israelites of the New Covenant.[9] His ministry and writings had a great impact in Russia and Europe and were known around the world.

In 1888, Rabinowitz said, "I have two subjects with which I am absorbed—the one, the Lord Jesus Christ, and the other, Israel."[10] A year later while visiting London, he said: "Russia is like the ocean, the Jews there are like shipwrecked people, and since, by God's mercy, my feet are on the Rock (which is Jesus) . . . I am shouting and signaling to my shipwrecked people to flee to the Rock."[11]

The establishment of Rabinowitz's Messianic congregation in Kishinev marks the beginning of the time of fishers sent to the Jewish people in Europe, and specifically in the Land of the North. It was the start of a great paradigm shift!

Herzl Dreams of A Sovereign Jewish State

Fourteen years after Rabinowitz viewed the life-changing sunset in Jerusalem's Garden of Olives, Theodor Herzl, a Jewish attorney and writer, penned an essay titled, "Der Judenstaat" (*The Jewish State*). That essay, published in 1896 and subtitled, "An Attempt at a Modern Solution to the Jewish Question," changed the course of Jewish history. Herzl dreamed of reestablishing a sovereign Jewish state on Jewish soil. Under the prophetic anointing of a true fisher from God (God can speak prophetically through anyone He chooses), Herzl wrote:

> In the world as it is now, and for an indefinite period will probably remain, might precedes right. It is useless, therefore, for us to be loyal patriots, as were the Huguenots, who were forced to emigrate. If we could only be left in peace . . . but I think we shall not be left in peace. . . .[12]
>
> The idea [of a Jewish State] must radiate out until it reaches the last wretched nests of our people. They will awaken out of their dull brooding. Then a new meaning will come into the lives of all of us. . . .
>
> Therefore, I believe that a wondrous generation of Jews will spring into existence; the Maccabees will rise again . . . and we shall at last live as free men on our own soil, and die peacefully in our own homes.[13]

In 1897, Herzl orchestrated the first worldwide gathering of Jews since A.D. 70. The delegates to this Zionist Congress, held in Basel, Switzerland, established the World Zionist Organization. Herzl became its first president. (Amazingly, I was in Basel in the fall of 1997, 100 years to the day after the Zionist Congress first met. I spoke at a prophetic conference held within blocks of the site where Herzl and his Jewish friends gathered.)

Zionist Congress Meets in Basel

In his inaugural address, Herzl prophesied, "We are here to lay the foundation stone of the house *which is to shelter* the Jewish Nation."[14] In his diary entry for September 3, 1897, shortly after he returned from the Zionist Congress, Herzl went one step further and declared:

This memorial in Israel stands in honor of a man who gave his life in an attempt to save the lives of 117 Jewish children in Europe.

Were I to sum up the Basel Congress in a few words—which I shall guard against pronouncing publicly—it would be this: "At Basel I founded the Jewish State."

If I said this out loud today I would be answered by universal laughter. Perhaps in five years, and certainly in fifty, everyone will know it.[15]

God raised up and released fishers to pursue and save the Jewish people in both the religious and secular realms. Both Rabinowitz and Herzl brought hope and direction to their people, but the work of Rabinowitz revealed the greater plan of the God of Abraham, Isaac and Israel.

The shadows of World War I settled on the nations of the world even as God's fishers began to draw His people back to their biblical homeland. Yet the borders and gates of Israel remained in the antagonistic grip of the Turks until God supernaturally put down one national power and exalted another.

During the war, Britain ran out of acetone, a component used to gelatinize a highly explosive mixture of nitroglycerin, guncotton and a petroleum substance called cordite. Cordite was the primary element of explosives at that time.[16]

Until war broke out, Britain had purchased all of its acetone from Germany, now its principal enemy. The acetone shortage literally put the entire nation at risk. In desperation, Winston Churchill, then the first lord of the admiralty, summoned a brilliant Jewish chemist named Chaim Weizmann to the British War Office. He asked him to develop a synthetic version of cordite that did not require acetone and placed every available government facility at his disposal.

Britain Battles for Palestine

While British forces under General Edmund Allenby battled Turkish troops for control of Palestine, Dr. Weizmann developed and produced 30,000 tons of an acetone-free synthetic cordite that was even more explosive than the original version! When Weizmann was asked what he wanted in return for his vital service to Great Britain, he said, "*If Britain wins the battle for Palestine*, I ask for a national home for my people in their ancient land."[17] Chaim Weizmann would later become the first president of the reborn nation of Israel.[18]

Weizmann received his answer on November 2, 1917, when British Foreign Minister Arthur James Balfour issued a statement on behalf of the British government, with the approval of the Cabinet:

> His Majesty's Government views with favour the establishment in Palestine of a national home for the Jewish people, and will use their best endeavors to facilitate the achievement of this object, it being clearly understood that nothing shall be done which may prejudice the civil and religious rights of existing non-Jewish communities in Palestine, or the rights and political status enjoyed by Jews in any other country.[19]

British Troops Take Jerusalem

Through a miracle, General Allenby, on December 11, 1917, took possession of Jerusalem without firing a single shot. Before entering what is called the Old City, the general sent planes over Jerusalem during daylight hours to learn the size and deployment of the Turkish troops within its walls. He also had the planes drop leaflets calling for the Turks to surrender, and for some reason the Turkish forces fled the city during the night.

Author Ramon Bennett reported:

> The dropped leaflets, signed with the name of "Allenby," were taken by the Turkish Muslims to be a directive from "Allah" for them to leave the city. No shots were

fired in the capture of the Old City of Jerusalem. General Allenby, a devout Christian, would not ride his horse into the city. He dismounted, and cap in hand, led his horse and his troops into the City of the Great King.[20]

Britain finally forced Turkey to sign an armistice in October of 1918. The area the world called Palestine was in British hands. At the end of the war, Britain was given a mandate, or official authority, to administer most of the Middle East. After years of political maneuvering and high-level betrayals, more than 70 percent of the land promised to the Jewish people was placed in Arab hands and named "Trans-Jordan." Yet, there was One who remembered His promises to the Jewish people. He was unmoved by riches, politics or the schemes of men and nations; and His promises would come to pass.

The British government imposed severe immigration quotas on Jewish immigrants who wanted to go to the Promised Land. Yet, despite seemingly impossible obstacles, determined Zionist groups defied the quotas and established colonies in *Eretz Israel* ("the Land of Israel").

Russia Embraces Communism

The labor pangs grew stronger and more violent with each decade, signaling that birth was imminent. As always, the dragon of old waited and schemed to destroy the divine seed of God's will before its birth or immediately after delivery.

While the voices of many fishers such as Herzl raised the alarm of danger to the Jewish people in Germany, Russia and the Balkans, only a fraction of them heeded the warning. Meanwhile the world went through violent labor pangs of its own. The doctrines of Marx, Lenin and Trotsky ignited fires of violent change that in 1917 plunged Russia into the darkness of atheistic Communism, producing an ungodly broth in opposition to both Christians and Jews.

Germany struggled with economic and social woes of its own after its humiliating loss in World War I. A little-known man from Austria (born seven years after Rabinowitz had pondered the truth of the Messiah on the Mount of Olives), penned a journal of hate called *Mein Kampf*. He rapidly rose in Germany's political ranks on a wicked wave of anti-Semitism and his extremist nationalistic doctrine of Aryan Supremacy. He is another in a long line of historical examples of a hunter who has been released.

The man's name was Adolf Hitler. As his grip closed on the reins of the German government, nation after nation ignored Hitler and the Nazi phenomenon. Leader after leader overlooked the growing army of Brown Shirts that surrounded the Nazi kingpin. However, the One who never sleeps knew what was afoot. Once again He sent fishers to warn His people before the coming trauma was fully released.

Thousands Heed the Fishers

Jeb Zabotinsky was one such fisher. An early Jewish pioneer in Israel, in 1933 he traveled throughout Europe and Germany in particular, warning "There is no future for you here, come back to your land while the doors are still open."[21] Thousands heeded the admonitions of Zabotinsky and others to flee the North, but millions of Jewish people in Germany, Austria and the Balkan countries did not.

Hitler came into power that same year and issued the Nuremburg Decrees which denied Germany's Jews any legal or citizens' rights. In the years that followed, he removed more rights as he gained and consolidated power, first as Germany's chancellor, and then as Führer (literally "the leader").

While the world looked on, Hitler established five concentration camps for Jews within Germany's borders (they included two sites that would gain horrendous infamy: Buchenwald and Dachau).[22] He claimed that his actions were legal under international law since the camps dealt with an internal problem, having nothing to do with the citizens of other nations. Most world leaders accepted this argument, reasoning that the Jewish people had no country or government per se.

By 1938, Hitler felt his power was strong enough to defy world opinion on a larger scale, so he suddenly "annexed" neighboring Austria into his Third Reich in what was called the *Anschluss*. The book *Exodus II* aptly depicts the scene: "Overnight, Hitler did in Austria what took him five years to do in Germany. He took away all the rights of the Jewish people, confiscating their businesses and instituting his atrocities immediately."[23]

The League of Nations, the toothless precursor to the United Nations, had neither the power nor the will to stand up against the Austrian bully ruling Germany. When the League of Nations failed to act, American President Franklin D. Roosevelt called a meeting of national leaders. He wanted them to discuss ways to rescue the Jewish people from Germany and Austria.

Fifteen weeks after the taking of Austria, representatives of 32 nations met in Evian-Les-Bains, France. On July 6, 1938, the conferees argued for hours over which delegate would chair the meeting. Moreover, after two days of halfhearted wrangling, no nation, not even Great Britain or the United States, was willing to take in more than a token number of Jewish immigrants. Hitler sent spies to monitor the opinions and determinations of the nations represented in Evian.

Nazis Prompted Toward the Holocaust

According to author Steve Lightle, Hitler's spies reported to the Führer, "You can do anything you want to the Jews; the whole world does not want them." Lightle said that one German newspaper, referring to a Nazi plan to *sell* Jewish lives to the nations at the meeting, declared in a headline, "Jews For Sale, Who Wants Them? No One."[24]

Once Hitler's spies confirmed that none of the nations whose representatives met at Evian were prepared to protect or offer sanctuary to more than a few Jews from Germany, Austria or Eastern Europe, he knew nothing stood in the way of the "Final Solution." Evidently, the report also convinced Hitler that he was dealing with sheep, because less than two months later, Germany's armies engulfed Poland in a *blitzkrieg* or "lightning war" and catapulted the world into World War II.

Barely one month later, Germans went on a rampage of their own called *Kristallnacht* ("Crystal Night") during which they smashed the windows of synagogues, Jewish businesses and homes, marking the full-scale beginning of the Holocaust.

By 1942, Hitler was ready to expand his extermination of Jewish people beyond the borders of Germany and Austria to include all of Europe. At the Wannsee meeting in Berlin, he essentially authorized the total annihilation of the Jewish population in Europe, exactly as he envisioned in his demonically inspired book, *Mein Kampf.* The Nazi war machine brutally murdered 6 million defenseless European Jews before it was finally stopped in 1945. Pastor Ulf Eckman of Sweden wrote in his book *The Jews: People of the Future*:

> There are no words to describe the suffering it inflicted. It is impossible to depict the wretchedness and misery in its wake. That it was perpetrated at all is heinous. That it was committed by a nation that was considered the cultural elite of Europe, is incomprehensible; and that it was done by Christians, is a shame beyond words.[25]

First God sent Jewish and Gentile fishers to warn the Jewish people of their danger, but only an estimated 600,000 heeded the warning in time to flee. Once the hunters gained momentum, they exterminated two-thirds of the 9 million remaining Jews. Not one nation represented at the Evian meetings had clean hands. Nor, as we shall see in the next chapter, was the Church guiltless in this unspeakable tragedy.

In spite of the hatred that led to the massacre of 6 million Jewish victims, God still had a plan to restore His ancient Covenant People to their land. The world would learn firsthand that nothing and no one could stand in His way.

The nations of the world were shocked to see images of the atrocities carried out by Hitler's henchmen at German concentration camps in Buchenwald, Dachau and Bergen-Belsen. For a brief window of time after the end of World War II, people in most of the Allied countries softened their attitudes toward the Jewish people who survived the Holocaust.

FIGHTING THE "OTHER WAR"

Throughout World War II, the British had fought another war *against Jewish immigration* to the Promised Land! The Arabs conducted a nonstop campaign of vandalism and terrorism against Jewish settlers; so in self-defense, the settlers organized underground vigilante and defense groups such as the Irgun, the Stern Gang and the Hagana. At first, most of these groups limited their activities to defense only, but as Arab atrocities and British violence increased, the Jewish groups kept pace (especially the violent Stern Gang). The Hagana worked tirelessly to help rescue desperate refugees from the Holocaust in Europe, despite Britain's best efforts to stop them.

By 1947, the British occupation forces and the British people were so exhausted with the struggle that the Empire returned the "Palestine problem" to the United Nations. A UN committee was formed to investigate and eventually recommended to the General Assembly that the Promised Land be divided or "partitioned" equally between the Jews and the Arabs. What happened next could only be attributed to the intervention of God.

Russia, hungry for the petroleum reserves in the Middle East, desperately wanted to see Great Britain remove its military forces from the region. The best way to make that happen was to back Israel's desire for independence. In his book *The Miracle of Israel*, the late Gordon Lindsay, founder of Christ For The Nations, described what happened next:

> The Russians, witnessing Britain's dilemma, had secretly facilitated the migration of 100,000 refugees through central Europe. Soviet officials helped them get on ships at Black Sea ports. Andrei Gromyko, Soviet foreign deputy of the USSR, pled their case before the UN saying:
>
> > It would be unjust if we deny the Jews the right to realize these aspirations to a state of their own. During the last war, the Jewish people underwent indescribable suffering. Thousands are still behind barbed wire. The time has come to help these people not by words but deeds.
>
> Because the Russian bloc voted in favor of the Jews (vote 21-20), the Jews gained the right to plead their case before the UN.[26]

A Day for Jewish People to Rejoice

That day in that subcommittee marked the first time in UN history that the USSR and the United States ever jointly supported a major decision! Finally, the Partition Plan came to a vote in the General Assembly where a two-thirds majority was needed for passage. Jewish people in Israel and around the world kept their ears glued to their radios. The resolution passed on November 29, 1947, and Jewish people around the world danced for joy.

Within three days, more than 40 million Arabs pitted themselves against the 600,000 Jews already living in Israel. Declaring a holy war or *jihad*, Arab leaders publicly vowed, "We are going to kill all Jews or drive them into the sea."[27] They were so confident that they warned all the Arabs who were living peacefully within the borders of the Jewish partition to move out of their homes for a few days until the Jews were wiped out. Ironically, this is the true origin of the Palestinian refugees.

The battle for survival went on for months during the time between the UN vote authorizing the partition of the Promised Land and the actual end of the British rule over the region. The British government did little to stop the violence, but it was careful to continue deporting every Jewish immigrant who did not have a visa. Only the determination and organization of the Hagana defenders saved the Jewish people from annihilation in their own land.

In the UN, opponents to the formation of a Jewish state worked feverishly to stop Israel from declaring independence, but they became entangled in red tape until past midnight.

Israel Becomes a Nation

At one minute past midnight, on May 15, 1948, the state of Israel came into being. While Israel's opponents continued to argue in the UN, they were interrupted with the announcement that U.S. President Harry S. Truman *officially recognized* the new state of Israel and extended full diplomatic privileges. The USSR, eager to make sure the British never returned to the Middle East, quickly recognized the nation of Israel as well![28]

While tiny Israel and its fledgling army of 6,000 men desperately prepared to face the armies of Jordan, Syria, Lebanon, Iraq, Saudi Arabia, Yemen and Egypt, her enemies successfully engineered a vote that made Jerusalem an international city controlled and administered by the UN. Gordon Lindsay wrote:

But on December 4, 1948, thousands gathered around the tomb of Herzl, raised their right hand and took the oath, "If I forget thee, O Jerusalem, let my right hand forget her cunning." Mr. David Ben-Gurion summed up the feelings of the people of Jerusalem and all Israel when he declared, "Israel's position on the question of Jerusalem found a clear and final expression in statements by the government and all parties of the Knesset [the Israeli equivalent of Congress or Parliament] on December 5. Jerusalem is an inseparable part of Israel and her eternal capital. No United Nations vote can alter this historic fact."[29]

This is Israel, the only nation on Earth to be born in a day through the supernatural intervention of God. He prepared the ancient home for His displaced Covenant People; now He is once again sending out fishers to forewarn the Jews dwelling in the Land of the North of a growing danger lurking in the land. The fishers are calling, "Come forth now! Come forth from the Land of the North!"

CHAPTER 3

TOUCHING THE APPLE OF GOD'S EYE

"Ho there! Flee from the land of the north," declares the Lord ;
"for I have dispersed you as the four winds of the heavens," declares the Lord.
"Ho, Zion! Escape, you who are living with the daughter of Babylon." For thus
says the Lord of hosts: "After glory He has sent me against the nations which
plunder you, for he who touches you touches the apple of His eye."

ZECHARIAH 2:6-8

Tom Hess, an international prayer leader and a modern-day fisher of God, remembers seeing an inscription on a wall in the Nazi death camp at Auschwitz quoting the philosopher Santayana: "He who does not learn from the lessons of history is doomed to repeat them."[1] This statement could almost qualify as a prophecy for the Church!

Virtually everyone has heard about the Holocaust of World War II in which Adolf Hitler and the Third Reich murdered 6 million Jewish people in cold blood. Few people know that professed Christians, as has happened many times throughout history, helped birth and carry out that organized murder! In fact, Hitler modeled some of his most heinous anti-Semitic schemes on official policies drafted centuries earlier by Roman Catholic and Protestant leaders.[2] Even though most Christians in Europe did not pull a trigger, release poison gas or burn the crime evidence; nearly all of them looked the other way. A few believers aided the Jewish people and some shared concentration camp cells and died alongside the Jews, but most did not.

Dr. Michael L. Brown, a theologian and Jewish disciple of the Messiah, quotes Eliezer Berkovits, a respected Jewish thinker, about the "moral and spiritual bankruptcy" of Christian religion and civilization:

> After nineteen centuries of Christianity, the extermination of six million Jews, among them one-and-a-half million children, carried out in cold blood in the very heart of Christian Europe, encouraged by the criminal silence of virtually all Christendom, including that of an infallible Holy Father in Rome, was the natural culmination of this bankruptcy. A straight line leads from the first act of oppression against the Jews and Judaism in the fourth century to the holocaust in the twentieth.[3]

At this writing, at the beginning of the twenty-first century, survivors of the Holocaust still live among us. They give vivid testimony to the horrors of modern anti-Semitism gone mad in many of the world's most "enlightened" European nations.

To our shame, some of the greatest Church leaders helped pave the way to death camps in places such as Auschwitz and Bergen. They did it through anti-Semitic writing and teaching. They underscored it by the sheer force of their influence from the pulpit. Everyone must join Jewish people today in remembering the Holocaust with the words *Never again!*"

CHURCH EDICT AGAINST THE JEWISH PEOPLE

When Berkovits mentioned the "first act of oppression" against the Jews by Christians in the fourth century, he was referring to an edict issued by the Roman Catholic Church in response to the doctrines of Saint John Chrysostem (347-407). This early Church father was the patriarch of Constantinople, yet he described the Jewish synagogue as "a place of meeting for the assassins of Christ . . . a den of thieves; a house of ill fame, a dwelling of iniquity, the refuge of devils, a gulf and abyss of perdition."[4]

Many scholars consider Chrysostem to be one of the greatest and most compassionate Church fathers. Yet the writings of this renowned saint reveal at least one very dangerous flaw. He said, "As for me, I hate the synagogue. . . . I hate the Jews."[5] Ironically, Chrysostem's name literally means "golden-mouthed." He used his gifts of persuasion to birth the Christian doctrine (popular even in this century) that anyone who persecuted the Jews was acting as an "instrument of Divine wrath."[6]

Anti-Semitic Rhetoric Spreads
A who's who of Church leaders and thinkers echoed Chrysostem's sentiments in an avalanche of anti-Semitic rhetoric. These leaders included Eusebius of Cesarea, Gregory of Nyssa, Augustine and Jerome.[7] During the dark years that followed, many Jewish people living under the shadow of the Christian church of that day were forced to be baptized as Christians or face one of three dim choices: expulsion, torture or death.

In A.D. 327, the Church Council of Nicea declared that, for the benefit of Christianity, Jews could only exist "in seclusion and humiliation." Fourteen years later, Constantine II prohibited marriage between Christians and Jews.[8]

In 1095, Pope Urban II decided to help Emperor Alexius I of Byzantine to recruit knights from the West to battle the Turkish Empire. While presiding over a church council at the Cathedral of Clermont in France (the nation of his birth) in 1095, Pope Urban preached a fiery sermon to crowds outside of the cathedral and, on November 27, launched the First Crusade. He urged

During World War II, Hitler's S.S. troops gunned down 33,000 Jewish people at this site in Kiev known as Babi Yar, or Grandmother's Ravine.

his listeners to liberate the holy city of Jerusalem and offered them a spiritual reward:

> Whoever for devotion alone, not to gain honour or money, goes to Jerusalem to liberate the Church of God, can substitute this journey for all penance.[9]

Historian Bernard Hamilton said that when the pope finished his sermon, "the crowd shouted, 'God wills it, God wills it!' and surged forward to take the cross." The pope appointed a former knight who had become a priest to lead the crusade but events quickly spiraled out of control.[10] Armed with the pope's promise of forgiveness of past sins and "sins recently committed," nobles, knights, soldiers, farmers and housewives rallied to march on Jerusalem.

The Crusades Begin
The first assault was called the Peasant's Crusade because it was made by an unauthorized and poorly equipped army of mostly untrained peasants, including women. They were quickly defeated and most of its members were killed or enslaved.

The pope's promise was a strong incentive, however. Even soldiers who had been excommunicated from the Church were welcomed back to the fold with open arms if they made a vow to purge Jerusalem and the Middle East of all infidels. They were also released from any debt they owed to Jews and had blanket permission from the pontiff to rob the Jews on the journey to and from Jerusalem.[11]

Unfortunately, many of these crusaders decided to purge Europe of its own infidels by attacking any Jew they encountered on their journey to the Promised Land. John Hagee, the founder and pastor of the 16,000-member Cornerstone Church in San Antonio, Texas, writes, "On the First Crusade [there were a total of fifteen of them over a period of about 500 years] to the Holy

Land, the crusading armies left a trail of Jewish blood across Europe. Within a three-month period, 12,000 Jews were slaughtered in Germany as the crusaders screamed, 'The Jews have killed our Savior. They must convert or be killed.'"[12] According to Michael Brown, the leading slogan of the day throughout Europe was, "Kill a Jew and save your soul!"[13]

Pope Innocent III is considered one of the "saviors" of the Jews, and he did try to stop some of the killing in later years. Yet his writings clearly indicate that he also felt the Jewish people deserved to "wander over the face of the earth, without rights, except by gracious concession, without a home ... as if they were beings of an inferior species."[14]

Jerusalem Captured

The First Crusade successfully captured Jerusalem in the summer of 1099, but the crusaders spent their first week in the Holy City in an unholy slaughter of the Jews and Muslims in Jerusalem. One historian says the men who carried the cross into Jerusalem took Holy Communion and "heartily devoted the day to exterminating Jewish men, women, and children—killing more than 10,000."[15]

Is it any wonder that spiritual darkness blanketed the Church in the medieval period and beyond when it presumed to murder the Jews in the name of Christ?

In 1182, France expelled Jews from its borders and Austria did the same in 1421. After that, Jews were expelled from the cities of Cologne (1424), Augsburg (1439) and Mainz (1473). Warsaw, Poland, expelled its Jews in 1439, followed by Sicily (1492-93). Lithuania expelled Jews from its borders (1495), as did Portugal (1496-97) and Nuremburg (1499).[16]

These dates are important because they indicate that most of Europe was closed to Jewish people by the time the infamous Spanish Inquisition began in 1480. That means that Spain's Jewish refugees simply had no place to go.

How Jewish People Viewed the Messiah

It seems logical to assume that if Jesus wanted to convert mankind by force, He would not have gone through the agony of death on a cross. He could have simply commanded legions of angels to force every man, woman and child to bend their knees before Him. But our Savior does not resort to force. Instead, He allows us to choose whether to follow Him.

The Church has not done very well in following Jesus' example. History is strewn with examples of times when Christians condoned violence to either convert or eliminate those who did not believe. One of the Church's primary targets through the years has been Jewish people, and Jewish people have noticed.

In his book *Our Hands Are Stained with Blood*, Michael Brown translated the words of an Israeli writer who expressed the Jewish view of the way the Christian Church has portrayed the gospel of Christ to the Jew:

> Instead of bringing redemption to the Jews, the false Christian messiah has brought down on us base libels and expulsions, oppressive restrictions and burning of [our] holy books, devastations and destructions. Christianity, which professes to infuse the sick world with love and compassion, has fixed a course directly opposed to this lofty rhetoric. The voice of the blood of millions of our brothers cries out to us from the ground: "No! Christianity is not a religion of love but a religion of unfathomable hate! All history, from ancient times to our own day, is one continuous proof of the total bankruptcy of this religion in all its segments."[17]

This is not the model Jesus demonstrated to His followers. Jesus does not save the lost through force, coercion or military action. The Prince of Peace builds His kingdom with the weapons of love, grace and mercy. Religion at its worst forces its way through hatred, harshness and cruelty. Church leaders in nearly every century seem to miss this important point.

Why do I recount so many historical events? Because I am convinced that the history of the past that *we do not know* nearly always directly influences the way we think and view things in the present. Many Christian children grow up distrusting or disliking Jewish people from their earliest years, yet they cannot give a single substantial reason for their feelings. We should not be surprised to learn that many Jewish children are taught to distrust Gentiles, and Christians in particular. It is sad but true that history substantiates their fears.

Until the savagery of the Third Reich in the twentieth century, the Spanish Inquisition was the unrivaled pinnacle of Christian anti-Semitism in human history. Haman, the enemy of the Jews described in the book of Esther, seemed to take human form again in the person of friar Tomas de Torquemada, the pope's personally appointed grand inquisitor. Torquemada, whom we will meet again later in this chapter, was also the confessor to Queen Isabella, and he used the full powers of the Church and the Spanish crown to hunt down and persecute Jews. Ultimately, he wielded so much power in Spain that even the king and queen feared his disapproval.

SPAIN TARGETS ITS JEWISH CITIZENS

Spain's large population of Jewish people was the target of this unholy inquisition. The first Jewish people to visit Spain (called Tarshish in most instances) were presumably Israelite traders who negotiated the purchase and shipment of gold and silver for the construction of Solomon's Temple. The region became a safe haven for Jewish exiles following the invasion of Babylon and the destruction of Solomon's Temple.[18] Obadiah the prophet referred to these exiles and mentioned another name for Spain when he prophesied:

> And the exiles of this host of the sons of Israel, who are
> among the Canaanites as far as Zarephath, and *the exiles
> of Jerusalem who are in Sepharad* will possess the cities of
> the Negev (Obad. 1:20, emphasis added).

The *Doubleday Dictionary* identifies *Sepharad* with Spain and
describes the *Sephardim* as "the Spanish and Portuguese Jews or
their descendants."[19] Some historians believe these Sephardic
Jews helped found the nation of Spain sometime before the
birth of Christ. In any case, even more Jewish people fled to
Sepharad after the destruction of Herod's Temple in A.D. 70.[20]

Jewish people throughout the Roman Empire suffered even
more persecution than usual after Emperor Constantine converted to Christianity and named it the state religion.
Persecution against Jewish people intensified when the increas-
ingly influential Church fathers began to preach anti-Semitic
themes in their sermons, teachings and letters.

Christianity Declared Spain's State Religion

Then, in A.D. 586, a king named Reccared converted from
Arianism to Roman Catholicism, which was again declared the
state religion.[21] Given the clearly anti-Semitic stance of the
Church in that era, it was predictable that laws and decrees
directed against the Jewish people would increase dramatically.

During a series of Church councils, convened in Spain over
the next 125 years, the Jewish religion was virtually outlawed.
The Church required Jews to be baptized as Christians or be
reduced to the status of slaves, suffer the confiscation of their
property and see all of their children above the age of seven be
placed in Christian homes.[22]

Golden Age for Spain's Jews

In A.D. 711, African Moors gained power in Spain's southern
region and spread the influence of Islam. During this time,

ironically, the community of Spanish or Sephardic Jews enjoyed a golden age of economic, artistic and scientific achievement. Jewish people rose to the highest ranks of government and were honored for achievements in business, literature, the arts, the sciences and philosophy. In fact, many Jewish people from other Arab nations moved to Spain.

Christians, who had maintained power in the North, drove the Moors out of Toledo in 1085. While the Moors (with Berber reinforcements) and Christians sparred in Spain for nearly a century, the Jewish people never regained their position of power.

Some of these Jewish people trickled across the border to France. But they found opposition there, too. In 1235, the Council of Arles required Jews to wear a yellow circular patch (does this sound familiar?), and the Jewish people began to stand out from the French population in an unavoidable and dangerously conspicuous way.

Tide Again Turns Against the Jews

Problems for Jews in Spain accelerated after Pope Clement IV authorized the Spanish Inquisition to investigate the lives of Jews and Jewish people who had chosen to join the Church. Late in the fourteenth century, Spanish church leaders preached an increasing number of anti-Semitic messages, triggering such an epidemic of violence that in 1391, over a three-month period, 50,000 Spanish Jews were killed in a total of 70 communities.[23]

When Queen Isabella of Castile and King Ferdinand of Aragon united their kingdoms through marriage in 1479, they were concerned about the unyielding "Jewishness" of Jews who converted to Christianity to avoid death or persecution during previous persecutions from the Church. These Jews were called *converses* or *Marranos*, which means "pigs" in Spanish. They were equally hated by unconverted Jews and by the Church.

At the request of Ferdinand and Isabella, Pope Sixtus IV in 1480 established the office of inquisitor general and appointed Fray Tomas de Torquemada to the post.[24]

Church to the Jews: Convert or Leave

Spain's surviving Jews were given just four months to decide whether they wanted to leave the country or remain and join the Roman Catholic Church. As many as 400,000 abandoned their homes and businesses to flee Spain, after paying exorbitant exit taxes to officials. For some reason, 50,000 Jewish people decided to remain in Spain.[25] Many of them did not live very long.

Michael Brown reports in *Our Hands Are Stained with Blood*, "It is estimated that 30,000 Marranos were burned at the stake in Spanish Inquisitions from the fifteenth century until 1808. In addition to this, in 1492, all non-baptized Jews were expelled from the country."[26]

Jewish Offer to Columbus Nixed

According to Dr. Dell Sanchez, the pastor of a bilingual, multicultural church in San Antonio, Texas, there is historical evidence that on the night before Christopher Columbus set sail on his first voyage to the New World in 1492, Spain's King Ferdinand and Queen Isabella met privately with Minister of Finance Isaac Abranbanel and two wealthy nobles, Gabriel Rodriguez Sanchez and Santangel.[27]

These three influential men were Sephardic Jews, and they offered to underwrite the voyage of Columbus. They knew the royal coffers did not contain enough money to pay for Columbus's venture, even though the Jewish population had been taxed and their property largely confiscated by the Church and the crown for many years. In return for their investment, the three men begged the monarchs not to expel the Jewish people from Spain.

Just as the royal couple accepted the offer, the door burst open and the pope's grand inquisitor, friar Tomas de Torquemada, ran into the room waving a crucifix and screaming that "the blood of all Jews" would now be on the hands of the king and queen. Ferdinand and Isabella took the money, but reneged on their agreement. Instead of protecting the Jews, they issued a decree ordering the expulsion of all nonconverted Jews from Spain. This amounted to a death sentence since virtually all of Europe had already expelled Jews from their borders.

MONARCHS EXPORT THE INQUISITION

To make matters worse, the Spanish monarchs successfully exported their Inquisition and persecution of the Jewish people to Portugal, spelling the doom of thousands of Jews who had fled there. This anti-Semitic spirit was even exported to the New World where it would surface with deadly wickedness in Spanish territory in what is now Mexico, Texas and California.

Nothing matched the brutality and evil of the Spanish Inquisition, until Hitler and his Nazi henchmen. The Third Reich adopted and perfected the techniques and policies forged by Torquemada and the Church clerics of the medieval era.

In the face of such diabolic evil, God's Word stands unchanged and eternally true. It does not matter how many current events and impending crises become human history. We should never forget God's ominous warning to every human being, every human institution and every nation among men that he who touches Zion touches the apple of His eye (see Zech. 2:8).

Ulf Ekman quotes a question posed by a famous survivor of the Nazi death camps that expresses the way the victims of the Spanish Inquisition must have felt:

The [late] renowned Nazi hunter, Simon Wiesenthal, has described how he was rescued from the bullets of a firing squad. While he stood there in a line awaiting execution, and Jews died beside him, the soldiers suddenly stopped shooting. They had heard church bells, and took a break from the killing while they went to vespers.

How can a Jew who has gone through these things ever believe in a Christian again? Especially since the Christian church, Christian theologians and Christian countries have led the field in anti-Semitism.[28]

The answer cannot be found in a book of philosophy or in official public statements issued by churches or Christian groups. It is found in God's Word and in our active obedience to His commands concerning Jerusalem, Israel and the Jewish people. We begin with repentance, proceed with prayer and follow through with active deeds of intercession and love.

Jews in the North Face Another Crisis

In virtually every crisis leading to the persecution of the Jews, Christians have had an opportunity to step into the gap as fishers, to warn, encourage and assist their escape to safety or help them return to Israel. During the Holocaust, Corrie ten Boom and a few other Christians risked or lost their lives helping the Jews escape, but most Christians remained silent. Another crisis may loom ahead, this time in the Land of the North. *We can make a difference!*

A faithful generation of godly Christian pioneers and forerunners brought a message of warning and encouragement to the Jewish people in the 1970s and 1980s. This group includes Sid Roth, Gordon Lindsay, David Chernoff, Joel Chernoff, Dan Juster, Derek Prince, George Otis, Jack Hayford, Moishe Rosen (Jews for Jesus) and many others who found creative ways to touch the "apple of God's eye."

These men of God should be honored, and many continue to have influential and effective ministries. But a new generation must arise, put on the mantle and build upon the foundation that has been laid. The Church must face the issue of what God is doing among the Jewish people.

Our role as Christians is to pray and intercede for the Jewish people. We must do whatever God tells us to do, particularly to help them escape the Land of the North and return to their biblical homeland. We are destined to blow a trumpet and declare God's fresh purposes to this generation—whether the message is popular or not.

As Santayana was quoted on that death camp wall, we can learn from the mistakes of the past and prevent history from repeating itself. The Church repeatedly failed to demonstrate the love of Christ Jesus toward the Jewish people in times past, which produced disastrous results. Never again!

Our faithful prayers and righteous deeds must provide proof that we have recovered from our spiritual bankruptcy and now have more than enough of God's love to extend helping hands to the Jew. Our godly lives and gracious ways must draw a new line straight from the heart of the Messiah to the hearts of the Jews—even if they choose not to accept Christ as their Messiah once we have done these things.

We can no longer afford to look the other way. Our Master just will not have it. Our sermons, conversations and influence must be used to preserve and protect God's ancient Covenant People until they come to know their true Messiah. Our lives and conduct must model God's unconditional love for the Jews, not man's unreasoning hatred of those who seem "different." The challenge is that these things can only come to pass in the crucible of prayer, over the fire of obedience.

PART II

A RADICAL AND SUDDEN CHANGE—

A CONTEMPORARY MIRACLE

CHAPTER 4

WHEN THE WALLS CAME TUMBLING DOWN

How great are His signs and how mighty are His wonders!

DANIEL 4:3

I will never forget watching television reports of East German youth tearing down the Berlin Wall. Nearly delirious with joy, they swung sledgehammers, iron bars, chisels and anything else they could find. Emotions flowed freely in a frenzied attempt to topple the 12-foot walls that had separated Germany and imprisoned East Berlin for 28 years. It was an earth-shattering spectacle. It was historic!

The dramatic scene unfolded on Thursday, November 9, 1989, barely a month after East Germany had celebrated its 40th and final anniversary as a country. Major news organizations from around the world showed up after jubilant Germans began to disassemble sections of the 103-mile-long Berlin Wall. The border guards merely watched without interfering.

I remember participating in a prophetic gathering in Kansas City before the "wall came tumbling down" in which Paul Cain, a senior prophetic statesman in our generation, announced that "communism was going to be commun*wasm*." Sure enough, that prophetic word was fulfilled and the Wall was removed. I now possess a piece of the Berlin Wall that I acquired during one of my intercessory visits to Berlin. I keep it as a reminder that in God, all things are subject to change.

The fall of the Berlin Wall signaled the inevitable collapse of the Communist regime that overshadowed Russia and its satellite states. Day by day, people around the world watched as the Soviet machine disintegrated.

Finally, approximately two years later, we learned that Soviet leader Mikhail Gorbachev would step aside and the Soviet Union as we knew it was no more. Newly chosen president Boris Yeltsin and the Commonwealth of Independent States (CIS) took the lead,[1] 75 years after Communism seized power under the atheistic direction of Lenin. (See Appendix 2 for an overview of Russian history.)

There Was Another Wall That Fell

The Berlin Wall was not the first fortress around a city to tumble. Centuries ago another bulwark fell, sending shockwaves of catastrophic change throughout the nations. That event, too, signaled convulsive change in the affairs of mankind and in the balance of power over the world's most contested real estate.

> Now Jericho was tightly shut because of the sons of Israel; no one went out and no one came in. The LORD said to Joshua, "See, I have given Jericho into your hand, with its king and the valiant warriors. You shall march around the city, all the men of war circling the city once. You shall do so for six days. Also seven priests shall carry seven trumpets of rams' horns before the ark; then on the seventh day you shall march around the city seven times, and the priests shall blow the trumpets. It shall be that when they make a long blast with the ram's horn, and when you hear the sound of the trumpet, all the people shall shout with a great shout; and the wall of the city will fall down flat, and the people will go up every man straight ahead" (Josh. 6:1-5).

In a sense, the walls of Jericho were more formidable than the Berlin Wall. The Jericho rampart was wide enough for six chariots to run abreast at the same time. The walls were not designed to keep unarmed people *in*. They were designed to keep the strongest armies of men *out*. Yet, they fell. Why? Was it the force of arms or the fierce attacks of skilled soldiers that brought them down? No, they collapsed upon themselves under the power of what I call prophetic acts of prayer. In other words, they disintegrated in obedience to God's direct command.

Remember? The people went on a fast of criticism for seven days. They walked around in silence because God had told their leaders to do so. But then came a sound at the end of the seventh march on the seventh day. A shout of prophetic declaration arose from the people. The rest is history. *Believers of the one true God obeyed His command in faith and the impossible was made possible.*

The East German army erected the mighty Berlin Wall in 1961. It went up because, over a 12-year period, 2.7 million people had fled the nation into West Berlin.[2] At the end of World War II, Berlin was divided with West Germany controlling a portion. But the city lies completely within the borders of what was then East Germany. The Wall was built to keep the East Germans inside, not to protect them against dangers from the outside. This wall was fortified by armed soldiers, tanks, tank pits, machine guns, concertina wire and a whole slew of other devices. Yet not one bullet or tank shell was involved in its demise. What happened to bring it down? How could such a thing come to pass?

In actuality, the fall of the Wall was merely the final fruit of events that occurred beyond the realm or physical boundaries of the once-feared Iron Curtain, of which East Germany was a part. The Berlin Wall collapsed on itself because the demonic principalities and powers upholding the Iron Curtain were dislodged. This dramatic shift of power triggered an unprecedented movement of people across national borders.

THE TRUTH BEHIND THE FALL OF THE IRON CURTAIN

"God events" played a part in the fall of a modern superpower. Let's look back at a few of them.

A Christian Embassy Birthed in Israel

In a strategic public move, godly believers established the International Christian Embassy in Jerusalem with the goal of comforting God's people and summoning the Church to pray for Israel. On Passover 1980, the Embassy held its first of many Mordecai Outcry events to publicly expose the mistreatment and imprisonment of Russian Jews.

God simultaneously launched an invasion in the spirit realm. While God has always loved the Russian people and the many other people groups within the USSR, He had no love for the antichrist spirit motivating and sustaining the Communist regime. That government's dismal track record of persecuting Christians and Jews within its borders finally reached the point of no return in the heavenlies.

God Dispatches Prayer Commandos to Strategic Locations

God began to lead small groups of "prayer commandos" to strike from strategic places in the USSR at the root of key historical events that had launched evil into the world. He also sent prayer teams into East and West Germany to battle in the spirit realm.

The prayer commandos entered these nations armed only with the name of Jesus Christ, the Word of God, the power of the Holy Spirit and a divine commission to release prophetic prayers in strategic places. It was a replay of the battle between little David and the monolithic Goliath, who, at the time, ruled the North.

International intercessory prayer movement leaders Kjell Sjoberg, Johannes Facius, Steve Lightle and Gustav Scheller assembled a prayer conference in Jerusalem. Participants prayed for Israel and the release of Soviet Jewry. During the gathering, the Spirit set apart Lightle, Facius and two other intercessors for a prayer mission to the USSR.

One month after Soviet leader Mikhail Gorbachev took power, the four-person team arrived, commissioned with a mandate from Isaiah 62:10 to "go through the gates" of the USSR and prepare the way for the Russian Jews to return to their biblical homeland.

Commandos Pray in Russia

Team members also felt led to follow a strategy found in Zechariah 1:18-21. Dubbing themselves the "Four Smithskis" after the blacksmiths, or craftsmen, described in this passage, they set out in Jesus' name to "terrify the four horns of the nations that lifted up their hands against the land of Judah." (In both the Old and New Testaments, the term "horn" is often used to refer to the leaders or the power of nations or empires on the earth.)

In many of the USSR's Jewish centers, the team circled giant statues of Lenin, then proclaimed the idols would fall. The intercessors sought out key transportation locations along the "exodus route" to Israel and asked God to open up a highway of departure for the Jewish people who would leave the Land of the North.

The team went to the Potemkin Staircase, the gate of Odessa, a port city in Ukraine, which at the time was part of the Soviet empire. This famous staircase features a broad series of massive steps leading from the city's opera house in the city square to the waters of the Black Sea at the Port of Odessa.

Obeying the leading of the Lord, the four intercessors prayed in the Spirit as they walked up and down the staircase. The ever-present Communist secret police (KGB) followed them closely down the stairs, trying unsuccessfully to decipher their words. When the prayer team members reached the bottom of the staircase, they quickly turned around to retrace their steps. The red-faced secret agents were so close and surprised that they literally ran back up the stairs as fast as they could![3]

The Lord uses different people at different seasons. He always has His forerunners who go before and pave the way for others so that they too can take their turn carrying His baton in this prophetic relay race. Years later, Scheller and others watched the first shipload of Russian Jews leave for Israel from that very port. I, along with others, have stood on those same stairs in Odessa, at the edge of the Black Sea. As intercessory watchmen, we spoke forth that this port would remain open and we lifted up a cry, "Let My people go!"

"Invasion Mission" Launched

From late December 1985 to early January 1986, Facius and Lightle returned to the Soviet Union along with 12 other intercessors from a number of nations. This would be their most important and historic prayer assignment behind the Iron Curtain. It could be called an "invasion mission."

Their first assignment was to launch a "spiritual missile" at the office (specifically, the spiritual principality behind the office) of Soviet President Mikhail Gorbachev in the Kremlin.

On New Year's Eve 1985, during a bitterly cold afternoon, the 14 praying men marched double file "just like a commando unit carrying a spiritual missile." One of the intercessors had previously been to Gorbachev's office and was able to guide the others right to the target. Lightle later wrote about what happened:

> The sign to launch our missile was for me to take off my hat, although the wind was blowing and it was snowing. . . . I'll never forget what happened. It was wild, because we had to march like a commando unit, but God gave us tremendous joy. . . . As we were marching, we had big smiles on our faces. We turned the corner. . . . I had not

Statue in Prague

seen so many police, KGB and army people before. No Russian person walks down that sidewalk, but there we were. The KGB came running across the street, about forty or forty-five of them. They were stunned as they walked along with us. They didn't know what we were planning to do, but it didn't affect us a bit. When we got right in front [of the door leading to Mr. Gorbachev's office] to where I could reach out and touch the door, I took off my hat.[4]

While the men smiled at their anxious and confused KGB "escort" squad, they also spoke into the spirit realm and released a deadly missile from God's Word. It was the same word that brought down another king who dared to reject God's commands. Thousands of years earlier, Samuel the prophet had delivered that fatal missile from heaven, dislodging King Saul, a Jewish ruler who had misused his authority:

> Because you have rejected the word of the LORD, He has also rejected you from being king. . . . The LORD has torn the kingdom of Israel from you today and has given it to your neighbor, who is better than you (1 Sam. 15:23,28).

With the divine payload delivered to its target, the 14 contemporary commandos abruptly turned around and walked away from Gorbachev's office. Going back the way they had come, they left their bewildered and unsuspecting KGB escorts scratching their heads.

The Soviet Union Disappears
Six years later to the week, on Christmas day 1991, Scheller and his wife were watching television in Odessa, Ukraine. Gorbachev came on the air and announced, "I hereby discontinue my activ-

ities at the post of president of the Union of Soviet Socialist Republics." Scheller summed it up: "With him disappeared the Soviet Union."[5]

During the same trip, the prayer team also invaded Lenin's Tomb in Moscow. It is reported that many Russians had called the tomb holy even though they did not believe in God.

Through divine intervention, the intercessors found themselves alone in what amounted to one of the Soviet Union's most "holy" shrines to the spirit of death. For decades, line after line of schoolchildren were brought to that tomb to honor the spirit of death hovering over the remains of the father of the Communist revolution. On this day, God dispatched a commando team of prophetic intercessors to destroy the demonic power behind this idol.

The Lord miraculously arranged for the guards in the tomb to be distracted. Responding to a problem outside of the shrine, they rushed away, leaving the team alone to drop their "bomb" in the Spirit. As team members encircled the decaying body of Lenin encased in glass, they broke the power *of the spirit of death in that place* in the name of Jesus Christ.[6]

Hess Focuses on Russian Jews

In the 1980s, Tom Hess led a 24-hour Prayer Watch in Washington, D.C. I often joined Hess in his Supreme Court Prayer Watch in the nation's capital and called for God's intervention through prayer and fasting. Hess has since taken an assignment to lead the Jerusalem House of Prayer for All Nations on the Mount of Olives, and Dick Simmons, of Men For Nations, one of my mentors, now leads prayer and intercession for our nation on Hess's former site.

In 1985, Hess led a team to Egypt and Israel. While praying for the Jewish people on Mount Sinai, the Holy Spirit told Hess he was to go to America and Russia to help prepare for the future exodus.

In late 1986, Hess felt he was to take a team of 38 Jewish and Gentile believers on a prayer journey to Russia. They were greeted at the Leningrad airport by the KGB, but later they managed to meet with and encourage Russian Jewish dissidents called refuseniks (see chapter 5 for further information on refuseniks). The team traveled to Moscow and completed a prophetic Jericho March around the Kremlin. While at Red Square, they prayed for the release of the Jewish people living within the borders of the Soviet Union.

On Yom Kippur, the team visited a Jewish synagogue in Moscow, where they provided clothing and Bibles to many Russian Jews. Members also serenaded their KGB escorts with "O Come Let Us Adore Him," something neither group will ever forget.

This strategic visit took place simultaneously with the summit meeting in Iceland between U.S. President Ronald Reagan and Gorbachev. When Hess's group finally reached Jerusalem they stood on the Mount of Olives and issued a prophetic command to the Land of the North to release the Jewish people, in the name of the Lord. Within a few days, the Soviet Union unexpectedly agreed to within one year release 12,000 Jews who wanted to immigrate to Israel.[7]

The Second Prayer Mission

Hess led a second prayer mission to the USSR in the spring of 1987, with a specific assignment to strike at the root of the communistic ideology that at the time had enslaved virtually 70 percent of the human race. In Moscow, God ministered to the group from Daniel 12:1, revealing that Michael was arising to deliver the Jewish people out of the Soviet Union. It was no coincidence when they went to a major museum in the Kremlin called The Church of Michael the Archangel and prayed for the deliverance of the Jews.[8]

The team marched Jericho-style around the Kremlin. Then they moved on to Leningrad to visit an atheistic museum, housed in an old church building that was converted into an anti-God memorial. On the lower floor of the church, there was displayed a statue of a large, nude male figure surrounded by little cherubs or demons and an eerie portrait of Lenin. These items aptly portrayed the god of Communism. Hess described the twisted scene in detail and explained what God sent the prayer team to accomplish:

> The central focus is a picture of Lenin with all the religions and cultures of the world being subjugated by communism. The cross is broken in two. The American, British, Swiss and other flags are torn in two and the hammer and sickle triumph over the world. We did another Jericho march around the atheistic museum, and with the Sword of the Spirit laid the axe to the spiritual root of communism in the very city where Lenin instituted this demonic ideology in 1917.[9]

By the turn of the century, Hess had led 10 teams of Jericho-type prayer marches in Russia. Today he is setting his sights toward organizing similar on-site prayer ventures in other lands.

Canceling the Soviet Constitution

Lightle also took a 12-member prayer team to Moscow on the 70th anniversary of the Bolshevik Revolution of 1917. The holiday commemorates the date when Lenin signed the constitution of what became the USSR. The prayer team's heavenly mission was clear and seemingly impossible: They were sent to *cancel* the Soviet Constitution signed by Lenin and rewrite a new one based on God's Word!

After a series of adventures, the 12 prayer commandos gathered in a circle in front of the building where Lenin signed the constitution into law (the building now houses the Bolshoi Theatre). The four KGB agents tailing them were so desperate to learn their plans that one of them accidentally poked Lightle in the back with his elbow as he strained to understand their words and another was literally cupping his hands to his ears to hear! Lightle wrote, "I don't know why he was doing that, I was praying in the Holy Spirit and I know he couldn't understand that."[10]

As I taught in my first book, *The Lost Art of Intercession,* "What goes up, must come down!" The prayers ascending from a radical remnant of the Body of Christ must have filled to the brim a golden bowl in heaven and started to overflow back down to Earth. Many believe the answers to these prayers started to appear in 1988 when Gorbachev changed part of the Soviet Constitution and initiated a total rewrite one year later. By 1990, Russian Jews were already immigrating in unprecedented numbers; but the best was yet to come.

God had one more assignment for the commando prayer team. Because "the Pharaoh of the North," Gorbachev, refused to give up God's people, the Jews, God had revealed to the intercessors that He was going to shake up the world economy, especially the economy of the Soviet Union and the Communist bloc nations.

Armed with a prophetic word and a key Scripture passage from Ezekiel, the team visited the Econocom Building (roughly the Soviet equivalent of America's Wall Street financial district). On the night of October 17, 1987, the intercessors "prayed judgment concerning the finances of the world, especially in the Communist bloc countries."

Lightle wrote, "When we left the Soviet Union and found out about the stock market crash on Monday, October 19, we understood our prayer."[11]

At that same season, I was participating with an intercessory team in New York City. The Lord had given me a vivid dream of a crash on Wall Street with the words, "When Wall Street hits 2600, this is a demarcation. Count 40 days after." Of course, in a global economy what happens on Wall Street reverberates around the world.

By divine direction, we were now interceding in New York City exactly 40 days prior to the great fall. We had spent hours in prayer that day and then felt released to go on site at the New York Stock Exchange. As we stood in the encased glass balcony overlooking the trading floor, we began to intercede. Then, like an arrow shot from its bow, a prayer was released that hit the target, and we all knew it.

At that moment, the time clock changed to 1:26:00 p.m., while at the same time the trading hit 2,600. Isn't it amazing to see how God can orchestrate these things? Then, just as the dream had stated, we began to "count 40 days after." Sure enough, 40 days later the U.S. stock market suffered a devastating but temporary crash. Interesting, isn't it? The Lord had people who did not know one another, and who were in two different parts of the world, engaged in the same prophetic intercessory activity!

Identificational Repentance in Evian

July 6, 1988, marked the 50th anniversary of the international travesty that took place in Evian, a small French town situated on the shores of beautiful Lake Geneva. As we discussed in chapter 2, it was there, half a century earlier, that leaders from 38 nations of the world met at the request of U.S. President Franklin D. Roosevelt. Though they started with good intentions, they ultimately failed to properly answer the question, How do we rescue the Jewish people out of Germany and Austria? As a result, 6 million Jews perished at the hands of the mad Austrian dictator, Adolf Hitler.

Fifty years later, in what may be seen as a prophetic "year of jubilee" for the beleaguered Jewish people, intercessory and prophetic leaders representing each of the 38 nations that sent delegates to Evian in 1938, assembled for a prayer conference in Berlin. A small group of them also went to Evian.

The prophetic delegates met together under a mandate of God to conduct solemn acts of "identificational repentance" in Christ's name for the sins committed 50 years earlier against the Jews.[12] They were to restore the breach created when their fathers, mothers, forefathers, nations—and even the Church itself—forsook the Jews of Germany and Austria in their hour of greatest need.

I ardently wanted to participate in those gatherings because the Lord had placed these issues on my heart years before. Moreover, He had given me a personal mandate to teach and impart to others many of the truths concerning identificational intercession and repentance, which resulted in my writing the book *Father Forgive Us!*

The problem was that my wife, Michal Ann, was nine-and-a-half months pregnant with our third child. With the birth of our child two weeks past due, I was not able to attend. Instead, I opted to intercede at the same hour the delegates began to gather and pray in Berlin.

At 1:17 in the morning, I was praying in my living room in Kansas City, Missouri, confessing the sin American Christians committed when they failed to raise their voices on behalf of the Jewish people in 1939. The intercessors in Berlin were dealing with the same subject at about the same hour.

While I was in prayer, an angel appeared and stood in the doorway of the living room! The angel was dressed in a military uniform, and it looked right at me.

Many different things were revealed in that supernatural encounter that I will not go into at this point, but finally the angel said, "It is time for you to go and lay your hands upon your wife and call forth your son, Tyler Hamilton."

My conviction was that the angelic message was referring to something more and greater than simply the birth of my son, as important and wonderful as that was. The angel arrayed in a military uniform was sent to tell me that it was a time of birthing and it was a time of war.

Sure enough, when I laid hands on Michal Ann, she started to have contractions and our child was born hours later—*on 7-7-88*. Seven is the number of completion and eight is the number of new beginnings. On this day we had doubles! In both the natural and the spiritual realm, it was a pivotal day of completion followed by new beginnings, new openings and birthing. *Birth happens once the birth canal is opened.*

The solemn acts of identification, intercession and repentance of the Church on behalf of our historical sins against the Jewish people triggered a completion on the one hand and a "birthing" on the other. It closed the circle of pain and in a moment, released new freedom and life.

Just before the Berlin Wall fell, Soviet President Gorbachev visited East Germany and told German Chancellor Helmut Kohl that the Soviet Union had abandoned the Brezhnev Doctrine. Moscow would no longer use force to keep its satellite states from adopting democratic forms of government or free-market economies. This was an unprecedented miracle.

THE IRON CURTAIN STARTS TO FALL

By September 11, neighboring Hungary had pulled down the Iron Curtain around its borders, and within six months, 220,000 East Germans fled to the West through Austria or sought political asylum in West German embassies in Hungary. To put this in perspective, before the miracle of 1989 only a few East Germans managed to escape to West Berlin and at least 80 people died trying to flee.[13]

The fall of the Iron Curtain had an even greater effect on the immigration of Russian Jews to Israel and Western nations. Russia had a long history of anti-Semitism, but an invisible line was crossed when Soviet leaders chose to persecute the Jewish people living under their control and to deny immigration to Israel.

The refuseniks received worldwide coverage when they opted to risk life and limb to protest the bureaucratic denial of their applications for immigration. Russian Jews knew that simply by applying to leave the USSR for Israel they would probably lose their jobs, be denied basic privileges and endure harassment from the KGB and local Communist officials. They also realized that they could possibly face prison time. Nevertheless, thousands of refuseniks applied. They had *Eretz Israel* on their minds and in their hearts.

The Berlin Wall Comes Down

Sixteen months after the acts of identificational repentance were made before God in Berlin and Evian, the Berlin Wall came down.[14] The Iron Curtain of the Soviet Union followed. It marked the beginning of a remarkable decade in which Russian Jews could freely return to Israel. More than 1 million Russian-speaking Jews have moved from the former Soviet Union to the Promised Land, where Russian is now the second most common spoken language.

Just as it did in Jericho of old, amazing things happen when God partners with man and when man partners with God. Even walls called immovable start tumbling down!

CHAPTER 5

ACTS BEHIND THE SCENES

The people who know their God will display strength and take action.

DANIEL 11:32

Dismay and discouragement often overtake anyone who is brave enough to read accounts of the Spanish Inquisition and the World War II Holocaust. Something inside seems to wilt, and we can feel powerless to deal with such malodorous hatred.

Do not accept the temptation to give up!

The adage "Prayer changes things" is more than a trite phrase, a willful wish or another powerless Christian cliché. I know that on the surface prayer seems like an incredibly ineffective weapon in the face of such malignant hatred and violence toward the Jewish people. Yet, I am convinced that if we ever realize the *true power* of Spirit-directed and Spirit-inspired prayer, we would be shocked.

Picture all of the water in the Great Lakes combined with the immeasurable volume of the Pacific and Atlantic Oceans. Imagine all of that watery force held in check behind the trembling walls of a single massive dam by heavily reinforced metal floodgates measuring 10 miles or more in height.

Now envision a single control button wired to the opening mechanism of this great dam. Even a little toddler would have the strength to release the waters with one expeditious touch, flooding the earth with a deluge matching or surpassing that of Noah's day.

In the same way, the significance of the power of prayer is not based upon the strength or ability of the person praying.

Rather, it is rooted in the immeasurable power of God and the awesome force He releases in response to fervent intercession. As the Scriptures declare, "The effective prayer of a righteous man can accomplish much" (Jas. 5:16).

WHAT HAPPENS BEFORE A WALL FALLS?

Supernatural behind-the-scenes acts of intercessory prayer and prophetic proclamation at God's direction always precede the crumbling of walls, both in the natural and spiritual realms.

The walls of Jericho fell flat after seven priests with ram's horns led the people of God in a silent march around that pagan citadel for six days, and ended the silent siege on the seventh day with a long trumpet blast and a corporate shout. They did it all in obedience to the prophetic direction of almighty God.

In the same way, I believe the seemingly invincible Iron Curtain and the Berlin Wall collapsed because the people of God on both sides of the curtain obeyed specific prophetic directions and, over many years, conducted prayerful behind-the-scenes acts. We can now peek *behind* the curtain of history and see how God answered our prayers. It is time to give honor to prayer veterans such as the late Gustav Scheller, with Operation Exodus; Steve Lightle of Exodus II; Tom Hess, with The Jerusalem House of Prayer; and many others who laid a foundation of prayer through their pioneer works of rescue and deliverance in Christ's name.

Steve Lightle: Let My People Go!

In 1974, Jewish-American businessman Steve Lightle closeted himself away in a fourth-floor room of a Christian drug and alcohol rehabilitation center called Kaffestube, in Braunschweig, West Germany. He had already spent several years in Christian ministry in Europe, including a one-year stint at Kaffestube, but something was stirring in his soul. He made up his mind that he would fast and pray until one of two things happened: Either God would change him or he would die in that room.

For six and one half days Lightle prayed, fasted and was visited by angels. Then Jesus appeared in the room and deeply cleansed Lightle's heart, preparing him for a specific task. Lightle received a vision that pointed to a dramatic change in the spiritual climate of Europe. In a book titled *Exodus II: Let My People Go!,* he described his vision:

> I saw a lot of people and I recognized that they were Jewish faces. And there were so many! Then from a particular viewpoint, I could see that there was a multitude of Jewish people—hundreds and hundreds of thousands of them.
>
> Then my angle of vision changed again. This time I saw it from a height that enabled me to see the nation they were in. It was the Soviet Union, and these were Jewish people that were being gathered from different parts of that nation. On many small streets they were gathering from various regions of Russia. They were coming together and began to walk upon a big super highway that God had built that was bound westward. Somehow I knew that this was a highway that only certain people could walk on. Only those that God permitted could get on it. And as they walked, they began to come forth out of the USSR.
>
> At the same time there were ministries that God raised up that were as great or even greater than that of Moses in Egypt. And they began to proclaim unto the Soviet authorities, "Thus saith the Lord God of Israel, let My people go!" And the Soviets refused. Then God, through these ministries, brought great judgment upon the Soviet Union. The catastrophes were so severe that the whole nation was brought to its knees. Then it was as

though the Soviet Union coughed up the Jewish people and they began to walk on this specially built highway.

As I watched, I saw that the highway continued on through Poland, through Warsaw. It continued on through East Germany, through the city of Berlin. From Berlin it crossed over the border into West Germany at Helmstadt into the city of Braunschweig. This highway that had been built by God continued on to the city of Hanover and then into Holland where the Jewish people got on ships and went to Israel.[1]

During the following six years, Lightle shared what he had seen only a few times. In 1982, the Lord permitted him to publicly disclose his vision of a Second Great Exodus of the Jewish people from foreign lands to Israel. That is when he discovered that God had been revealing similar messages to Christians around the globe. The message had such great impact that radio and television reporters around the world sought him out for interviews.

When Lightle was finally released to share his experiences in *Exodus II: Let My People Go!*, he wrote, "Right now, in 1983, the Soviet Union has essentially closed all doors so that hardly any of the 2.5 million Jews [living there at the time] are able to return to the land of promise. But God will provoke the 'land of the north' to let His people go. The original exodus out of Egypt will seem like just a shadow of the upcoming dramatic events. No one will talk about the former exodus anymore because of the worldwide impact of the final one."[2]

God Releases Prayer Commando Teams

God began to give specific "prayer assignments" to intercessors around the world. Groups of "prayer commandos" began to travel to key places behind the Iron Curtain to lift up specific prayers and make prophetic declarations at the leading of the Holy Spirit.

A Russian statue depicting a posture of prayer.

In 1982, God intervened in the life of Swiss travel executive Gustav Scheller, who lived in England at the time. Over dinner in a restaurant in northern England, a doctor mentioned to Scheller and his wife, Elsa, that he had just returned from a Festival of Tabernacles celebration in Jerusalem where he heard Lightle speak of a second exodus of the Jews. Scheller had been reading the prophets in the Old Testament, and his heart leapt when he heard about Lightle's vision.

Two weeks later, the Schellers flew to Jerusalem. They wanted to talk with Lightle, but did not know how to contact him. That was not a problem for God. While out on a walk in Jerusalem, the Schellers spotted Lightle. It was a divine appointment with international implications.

The Schellers went on to work with Lightle in the early 1980s. They spread the news throughout the United Kingdom that God planned to return Jews living in the Land of the North to Israel. With the Cold War still at full throttle, they faced formidable skepticism in the media and even in the Church.

When they held a news conference at the Finnish parliament, the British Broadcasting Corporation (BBC) World Service carried Lightle's challenge across the globe: "It's time that somebody began to tell the leadership of the Soviet Union what the Word of the Lord says: Either they bow their knees to God, or God is going to judge them."

According to Scheller, a major Soviet newspaper mocked Lightle's declaration with the headline, "God Brings Russia to Its Knees."[3] The same God who once spoke through a donkey spoke prophetically through a Communist newspaper headline!

It was not long before the Soviet Union began to suffer some of the poorest grain harvests in its short history. The superpower tottered on the brink of bankruptcy and lost three leaders, Leonid Brezhnev, Yuri Andropov and Konstantin Chernenko, in just two and one-half years.[4]

The Impact of the Esther Fast

I suspect the upheaval in the Soviet Union was accelerated in part by a little-known prayer event called The Esther Fast Mandate. God planted the idea in the heart of Canadian minister Clyde Williamson during a churchwide, 40-day fast in January 1983. I never met this man, but I still have a copy of a small book he published called *The Esther Fast Mandate*.

The God-breathed vision captured in this little book had a lasting impact on my life. Here is a brief segment of the prophetic call God issued to the Church through Williamson:

> The Spirit of God is wooing people to do that which Queen Esther did in an absolute fast unto God, a fast in which to seek God for the restoration and deliverance of the people of Israel.
>
> And God shall give an appointed time and there shall be those in His body that shall set themselves aside without food and without drink for a period of three days that God will set forth out of bondage, His people (both Israel and the Church) from all over the globe. And they shall come forth by the thousands and by the millions and His name shall be glorified.[5]

Williamson served as a staff minister with Pastor Ralph Rutledge of Queensway Cathedral in Toronto, Ontario. The leadership team at Queensway concluded that *The Esther Fast Mandate* had to be committed to paper and distributed. It was not a one-time call for intervention through fasting, but a call for a yearly vigil, listing dates up to the year 2000.

The *Mandate* was hurriedly printed in the form of scrolls and distributed to contacts the church already had, but God had bigger plans. Within a short period of time, the news of the Esther Fast traveled around the world. Believers from 73 different nations joined together in a three-day fast for "the release,

return, restoration and revival of Israel and the Church."[6] Such
an international call to focused prayer was unprecedented, especially in those days when the worldwide prayer organizations we
have today did not exist.

Two Jewish holidays, Purim and Passover, occurred during
the Esther Fast that year. Jews set aside Purim as a time to
remember Esther's original fast which saved her people from
annihilation at Haman's hands. Passover, as we recounted in
chapter 1, honors the night God released the Jews from captivity in Egypt. The timing of the initial Esther Fast was crucial
because, at that time, the Soviet Union was allowing only 100
Jewish people per month to immigrate to Israel. Soviet officials
were cracking down on dissidents and they refused to approve
360,000 applications from Jewish citizens wishing to immigrate
to Israel. Moscow would not relent, despite growing pressure
from the United States and many other Western nations. Called
refuseniks, many if not most of the Jews who applied to make
aliyah experienced persecution, and many were imprisoned.

Tom Hess: Preparing the Way for Messiah

Tom Hess is another modern prayer pioneer appointed by God
for this day. He led seven prayer walks into Russia on behalf of
the Jews in the Soviet Union before the cloud of Communism
ever lifted from her borders and three more once the Iron
Curtain had fallen. During these walks, intercessors called out
for the release of the Jews from the Land of the North.

Hess also helped establish houses of prayer and prayer
watches around the world. He still conducts annual international prayer convocations in Jerusalem that draw people from
around the world. It has been my privilege to participate in some
of his historic behind-the-scenes prayer ventures as far back as
the mid-1980s. I am a witness to their incredible effectiveness.
Hess described two examples in his book, *The Watchmen: Being
Prepared and Preparing the Way for Messiah*:

[In Washington, D.C., in 1986,] I was fasting for a breakthrough in the United States Supreme Court because the Chief Justice was "pro-choice" on abortion (in favor of killing unborn babies). Someone said the results of my fast would be seen on television, which I found hard to believe. But one hour after I ended the fast, forty days later, the Chief Justice of the Supreme Court resigned, and God gave a pro-life Chief Justice and at the same time another pro-life Justice was appointed to the Court, to everyone's surprise. . . .

Another example was in Russia in 1986-1992—seven times in over seven years to do seven Jericho Marches around the Kremlin in Moscow, one every year. We saw tremendous breakthroughs: the year before we began only two hundred Jewish people had left Russia for Israel, but since then the wall of Communism came down and in the last ten years over 800,000 Jewish people have come home to Israel! There were numerous groups involved in 24-hour prayer watches, praying and fasting as we went there, and many were praying all over the world.[7]

Mahesh Chavda: Delivering a Prophetic Word

I have known Mahesh and Bonnie Chavda for more than a quarter of a century, and I consider them to be treasured friends and co-laborers in the ministry. The Chavdas have a powerful healing and evangelistic work, and they play a crucial role in the world prayer movement, leading the 600-plus Watch of the Lord gatherings that meet on Friday nights in various places around the world.

In 1986, the Lord told the Chavdas they were to deliver a prophetic word to the Jews behind the Iron Curtain. Mahesh Chavda traveled from Finland to Moscow. Risking discovery by the KGB, he spoke to refusenik leaders and delivered a prophetic word to an Orthodox Jewish rabbi. He said, "Thus saith the Lord, God is going to send a whirlwind of freedom, and this communistic pharaoh is going to let you go. God is going to set you free."[8]

The rabbi agreed that God might release his friends, but he assured Chavda that he would never be allowed to leave. Unmoved, Chavda said, "You're the leader, you're going to lead this people out. When the door is open, you take the people to Israel. This is the Word of the Lord."[9]

The rabbi told Chavda, "That's impossible, I'm a doctor of mathematics, and I build their rockets. Now I'm a rabbi, but because I know their secrets, they will never let me go." Chavda asked God to confirm His prophetic word and prayed, "O God of Abraham, Isaac and Jacob, show Yourself here." When he raised his hand, the rabbi nearly fell down under the power of God and exclaimed, "The pain is gone!" Chavda learned that the rabbi had been tortured by the KGB and had suffered from chronic rib pain until that moment.[10]

Two years later, Chavda was in Jerusalem to welcome home some of the first Russian Jews flown to Israel. The same rabbi's picture appeared on the front page of the local newspaper. He had finally made it to his ancient homeland. I like what Chavda wrote in his book: "For decades the Marxist communists had said, 'There is no God! There is no God!' Then one day the Lord stood up and said, 'There is no communism.'"[11]

In the years before the fall of the Berlin Wall and the collapse of the Iron Curtain, God supernaturally created a unique network of friends and built a worldwide "watch of the Lord." Then, with divine precision, He launched His secret prayer weapon against the gates of the enemy in the Soviet Union.

German Believers: Interceding Behind the Wall

God was also at work among believers in Germany during this season. My West German friend and Christian leader Michael

Schiffmann described to me some of the behind-the-scenes
events that took place in Germany between the end of World
War II and the day the Berlin Wall came down. In a personal e-
mail message, he wrote:

> After the Second World War, the Federal Republic of
> Germany was founded; and because of the total break-
> down of trust, some born-again Christians became part
> of that first government. The whole government repent-
> ed for the deeds of the Nazi regime and the Holocaust in
> one of their first constitutional meetings.
>
> In the fifties and sixties, the Lutheran Order of the
> Sisters of Mary took a strong stand for identificational
> repentance in particular for the Holocaust and initiated
> several public acts on those issues. Many churches
> responded [through] identificational repentance in their
> services during the sixties.
>
> In the early seventies, a movie that was broadcast
> called "Holocaust," made a deep impact into society and
> showed to the first generation after the war the depth of
> guilt and released a strong public awareness. This was
> followed by waves of identificational repentance that
> touched most denominations and most areas of West
> Germany.
>
> By the initiative of Ari Ben Israel, a Messianic Jew,
> and the German Intercessory Movement under the lead-
> ership of Berthold and Barbara Becker, together with
> many different national leaders, a conference was held
> that not only caught the attention of the secular media,
> but that was unique in wideness of range of the church-
> es and denominations attending.
>
> [In] 1985, at the very place [where the former
> German legislative assembly passed "racial laws" perse-
> cuting Jewish people before World War II], about 7,000

German Christians from 400 different cities [met] together with many representatives from Israel and with many victims of the Holocaust and some government officials. [They] made a public declaration of repentance and remorse that was spoken by all the participants. That very declaration was broadcast and watched by 30 million people.[12]

God worked stealthily through obedient believers from many nations, including some in East Germany, to prepare the nations and the Jewish people for the miracle He would soon work before our eyes. He even worked through political leaders such as President Ronald Reagan and British Prime Minister Margaret Thatcher who took such strong stands against the "evil empire" of Soviet rule.

Then there was the work of Pope John Paul II. What a wonderful contribution, both on spiritual and governmental fronts, was made by the man who heads the Roman Catholic Church—the church that had once led the charge against Jewish people during the Spanish Inquisition. Roman Catholics took the lead in calling for a freedom that would open the floodgates for Jewish people to return to Israel. No other pope has done as much as John Paul II to make restoration for the past sins of the Church.

Who but God knows the importance of each behind-the-scenes act of prayer, intercession, repentance or reconciliation that took place in the years before the fall of the Wall and the collapse of the Communist empire to the north? This much is clear: The labors of prayer and intercession we saw before the fall only foreshadowed even greater prayer assignments that would follow.

God Releases a Prayer Avalanche

God released one prayer avalanche to break through the walls, gates and obstructions blocking the return of the Jews to Israel from the Land of the North. This was the beginning of the fulfillment of the Scripture, "Thus says the Lord GOD, 'Behold, I will lift up My hand to the nations and set up My standard to the peoples; and they will bring your sons in their bosom, and your daughters will be carried on their shoulders'" (Isa. 49:22).

First we carried the Jewish people in the North on our shoulders through prayer and intercession. Then He released a different kind of flood to begin to break down centuries of betrayal, distrust and persecution of the Jews by self-proclaimed Christians. He anointed a remnant forerunner group to actually help carry the Jewish pilgrims back home through every means possible. This river of grace in the time of the fishers would require the Church to stretch out in repentance and serve others as never before.

Oh, let us, the broken and loving Body of the Messiah, carry the descendants of Abraham, Isaac and Jacob in our hearts as well as on our shoulders! Let us know our God, wax strong and release demonstrations by doing daring acts and mighty exploits for the glory of His great name in the earth!

CHAPTER 6

TRANSFORMATION: ALTERED STATES OF AFFAIRS

*Then it will happen on that day that the Lord will again recover the
second time with His hand the remnant of His people, who will remain,
from Assyria, Egypt, Pathros, Cush, Elam, Shinar, Hamath and
from the islands of the sea.*

ISAIAH 11:11

The collapse of the Soviet Union's suffocating curtain of terror
brought astounding transformations that still affect that region
and the world at large. Most significantly, from the moment the
Iron Curtain began to unravel, the number of Jewish immigrants making aliyah to their biblical homeland increased dramatically.

Before the beginning of the end, Russian Jews were rarely
allowed to emigrate; even though the Communist government
of the Soviet Union was historically hostile toward them and
openly treated them as second-class citizens. Just before the fall,
as few as 100 Jewish people were allowed to leave the Soviet
Union annually. The collapse of the Iron Curtain completely
changed the situation.

In the 13 months after December 1989, almost 200,000 *Olim*
("those going up") flooded out of the former Soviet Union to
Israel.[1] By June 2000, 1 million Jewish people had arrived in
Israel from the Land of the North. They fled for freedom in
automobiles, airplanes, trains, buses and ships. Most were assist-

ed by Jewish or Christian agencies, individuals and groups. It amounts to the emancipation and transportation of an entire people group from one part of the world to another. Nothing like it has ever happened on such a massive scale! But there are still far more we must reach and rescue.

THE EXODUS HAS BEGUN

Gustav Scheller and Steve Lightle met in Jerusalem in 1982. They grew closer as they prayed about ways to minister to the Jewish people in the Land of the North. They worked with several other intercessors and leaders to sponsor a prayer conference in Jerusalem in 1991. The first session began on the day the United States had set for Iraq to withdraw its troops from Kuwait.

Despite the danger of military conflict in the region, 120 believers from 24 nations bravely attended the conference to stand in the gap. War erupted that night. During a week punctuated by SCUD missile attacks and long hours wearing gas masks, God spoke to Scheller. He told him it was time to help bring the Jewish people home.

Scheller shared this with the leader of the conference, Johannes Facius, a Danish church leader and the coordinator of Intercessors International. Facius nodded in agreement. To their surprise, all 120 conference attendees concurred! Delegates donated $30,000 to finance the first flight of Operation Exodus to fly Russian Jews back to Israel. The flights continued with success, but Lightle, who headed the project, had received a vision years before that included ships as well as planes.[2]

Jews Leave Odessa by Ship
One year later, Lightle and Scheller formed the Exodus Shipping Line to transport even larger numbers of Olim to Israel from

Odessa, Ukraine. They entered complicated negotiations with Russian customs officials and Jewish Agency leaders from Israel, and then they negotiated with a Greek shipping company for the use of a large ship.

When the Soviet Union dissolved midway through the negotiation process, Lightle and Scheller had to start over again with newly independent Ukrainian customs officials. It did not matter—God had a plan and they were squarely in the middle of it.

In December 1991, the Exodus Shipping Line overcame every obstacle by God's grace. Lightle described the first trip: "At eleven minutes past midnight, the lines were cast off and we sailed out of Odessa with 476 Jewish immigrants making aliyah. This was the first ship since 1948 to take Jewish immigrants to Israel."[3] Many Exodus sailings followed taking thousands of Russian Jewish people home, from the Port of Odessa to Israel.

Each time a gap appeared in the "fisher's net" drawing these Jews of the northern diaspora home, new ministries appeared, as if on heavenly cue, to meet the need. Exobus appeared in June of 1991 to transport stranded Olim across Belarus from Kiev to the airport in Warsaw, Poland. From that beginning, Exobus expanded operations to 16 bases in four countries. At this writing, Exobus is carrying around 1,000 Olim a month to 13 airports in five countries.[4]

Refuseniks Stand Against Communist State

When the walls came down, a large number of refuseniks were ready to go. Most of these people of conscience lost their jobs and endured years of persecution simply because they had at one time applied for permission to immigrate to Israel. Year after year, the Soviet bureaucrats denied their requests. In most cases, the persecution extended into their places of employment and the local communities. Nevertheless, for years the refuseniks stood against oppression under the Communist regime. Many of them spent time in prison; most of them were Jewish.

When the Iron Curtain finally dropped, these Jewish survivors were eager to leave. The first to leave had prepared their official papers many years in advance and had lived "ready" for years. These people, for the most part, were clearly Jewish in their culture, bloodlines and religious belief.

However, many "second round" Jewish immigrants were barely identifiable as people of Jewish descent or faith. Some could not tell you who Abraham or Moses was. These descendants of Abraham were the product of a secular and anti-religious culture in which "being Jewish" evoked images of tattooed numbers on the skin. Since the era of the Russian tsars, many families had changed their Jewish-sounding names or hidden their Jewishness to avoid exile to the old tsarist Pale of Settlement, a community of isolation segregating Jews from the mainstream population.

In many cases it was difficult for these "hidden Jews" to prove their Jewish heritage. Corruption and organized crime in the former Soviet Union—particularly the forging of false identification and immigration papers—has made Israeli officials unwilling to accept many of the new identity papers held by Jewish people wanting to make aliyah.

JEWISH IMMIGRANTS: AN UNREACHED PEOPLE GROUP

Some have estimated that nearly 90 percent of the Jewish immigrants entering Israel are totally unreached by the gospel of Jesus Christ. Many are almost as ignorant of their Jewish heritage and religion. Christian ministries that work closely with Israel to help transport Russian Jewish immigrants to their homeland are careful not to evangelize the Olim. But there has been more freedom for the ministries working inside the former Soviet Union among the Russian Jews.

In 1990, before the collapse of the Communist government, Jonathan Bernis led a fact-finding mission to Saint Petersburg (then called Leningrad). The American pastor wanted to assess the condition of the Jewish people in the Soviet Union. During his visit, Bernis was struck by the spiritual hunger of the people he encountered.

Over the next two years, Bernis returned to the Soviet Union with other groups and helped establish a Messianic (Jewish Christian) congregation in Minsk. During these trips, the Holy Spirit began to speak to him about a unique ministry to the Jewish people in the Land of the North. He wrote in his foreword to Sandra Teplinski's book *Out of the Darkness*:

> By that time, the Iron Curtain had come down. Thousands of missionaries had poured into the former Soviet Union. Only a handful of them, however, were reaching out to the millions of Jews in the land.
>
> I knew God wanted to reach this remnant with the Good News—before they returned to the Promised Land. I also knew He was calling me to play a more significant role in the reaping. I didn't understand how I was to do this . . . then the idea for Messianic Jewish music festivals was born. I knew the Jewish people of Russia were greatly interested in Israel and the Jewish culture. I also knew that Russian people in general had a great love for music and the arts. Organizing a festival of Jewish music and dance seemed to offer the perfect platform for sharing the Good News in a Jewish way with the Russian people.[5]

Jonathan Bernis Launches Festivals in Russia

By May 1993, Jonathan Bernis had founded Hear O Israel Ministries (HOIM) and conducted the first Messianic music festival in Saint Petersburg at the Oktobersky Concert Hall. No one was prepared for what happened there. Bernis writes, "We had no idea what the results would be or how many people would come. So we were all shocked on opening night to find the 4,000-seat hall filled to overflowing."

Even more stunning was the scene following Bernis's short message and altar call: Over 50 percent of the crowd—half of them Jewish—rushed to the front of the concert hall to pray. Many on Bernis's team began to weep as they witnessed an outpouring of the Spirit not often matched in 2000 years since Jewish people became the first Christians in Jesus' day.[6]

HOIM, renamed the International Festivals of Jewish Worship and Dance, subsequently conducted 20 festivals, reaching more than 500,000 people in the former Soviet Union. Nearly half of those who attended the festivals were Jewish. The largest festival drew more than 60,000 people to the central football stadium in Odessa, Ukraine, in 1995. More than 200,000 people (approximately 80,000 of them Jewish) responded to altar calls at the festivals. In an e-mail correspondence, Bernis wrote, "God is at work among the Jewish people in a way that we have not witnessed since the first century."[7]

Prayer Assignment: Go to Russia

In the summer of 1994, David Fitzpatrick, Avner Boskey, Richard Glickstein and I participated in Bernis's third festival, which was convened in Minsk, the capital city of Belarus (White Russia). We had each been involved in different prayer groups that conducted prophetic intercession for Israel and the Jewish people. But for a season we would be a team with specific prayer assignments. Working hand in hand with Bernis and the festivals, we set out on a prophetic journey which crisscrossed Russia.

The Lord had a very specific assignment for this group, and a word. He told us that if we wanted to serve the Jews, we would have to do it *in Russia*. "This is not an optional trip, this is a strategic alignment," God revealed to me in a dream. That directive caught us off guard. While we all traveled a lot, relocating half a world away was not something we had envisioned. Nonetheless, we acted on this heavenly assignment. Fitzpatrick, Boskey and Glickstein actually moved with their families to Russia. I continued my task of intercession and networking stateside.

Our assignment was to pray that a way would be opened for the Jews to exit from the Land of the North and return to Israel. Belarus and the capital city of Minsk, in particular, marked part of the path leading from Russia to Israel through the great seaport of Odessa.

Most of the other routes required Jewish immigrants to take long detours or pass through nations and regions dominated by fundamentalist Muslims. Since ancient times, the path from the Black Sea through Ukraine and Belarus has been recognized as the southern gateway to Europe, a fact that was not overlooked by the Nazis during World War II. We learned that a lot of atrocities had been inflicted upon the Jews in Belarus. In preparation for the festival, we visited some of the sites.[8]

Preparing the Way in Minsk

We wanted to find a high place in the city where we could pray. A non-religious gentleman in Belarus suggested the Mound of Glory. We did not know what it was, but it seemed to make sense.

The Mound of Glory, as we discovered, was really a massive hill created by people who carried dirt one handful at a time in processions from their villages all over Belarus. The members of our prayer group walked up on this Mound of Glory and released specific prayers seeking a way of escape for the Jews in the Land of the North.

The day before the festival in Minsk was to begin, Bernis encountered significant resistance from local authorities.

Intercessory prayer by the entire festival team played a key role in the crisis, and God made a way where there was no way! In the end, local authorities asked if the festival could be extended another day to accommodate people who had been turned away from overflow crowds!

Minsk was just the beginning of our prayer team's intercessory cycle. During the next three years, we lifted up specific prayers for a variety of locations as God gave them to us.

Intercessors Visit a Synagogue

Once, traveling with a smaller prayer group, we went into Moscow from Minsk. There were three synagogues in Moscow, a city of 10 million people. The largest synagogue—the one the presidents and statesmen visit—was attended by only 200 to 250 people. The third synagogue had been firebombed about five months previous to our coming, and we felt that was the place we were to visit.

The sanctuary was boarded up and surrounded by a chain-link fence, but we felt we were to stay and pray. Eventually a couple of us jumped the fence and searched for the groundskeeper. When we found him, he opened up the facility and gave permission for the entire group to come in.

A Jewish brother from New York picked up something he spotted in the rubble of the burned-out building—amazingly, it was the complete history of the Exodus of the Jews, written in Russian. You can imagine what this meant to us, since we had come specifically to pray for a second and even greater exodus of the Jews from the Land of the North. During that trip God knit together the hearts of our prayer team members, which was composed of both Jewish and Gentile believers in Messiah.

Nazis Did Not Spare the Children

Other excursions with our Messianic Jewish friends took us to places such as Babi Yar (Grandmother's Ravine), a field across from Kiev's Jewish cemetery in Ukraine. On September 29, 1941, Nazi troops, assisted by willing Ukrainian soldiers, ordered the city's Jewish residents to strip off all of their clothing and line up in groups of 100. Mercilessly, the invading troops raised their machine guns and shot the helpless victims, one group at a time. The massacre lasted two days, as long as the gunmen had enough light to see their targets. Witnesses reported that the Nazis literally melted some of their gun barrels.

Thousands of small children, who were missed by the bullets of the Nazi machine guns, were simply thrown alive into the ravine of death and buried along with their murdered adult family members. Witnesses said so many victims were buried alive that the ground at Babi Yar literally moved for two days after the last gunshot was fired.

When the earth stopped trembling, 33,771 Jews were dead. Even the daily carnage count at the death camps in Treblinski and Auschwitz could not compare with the efficiency of the executioners in Kiev. However, the horror was not over. During the next year, 65,000 more civilians (mostly Jewish) were brought into Kiev from Nazi-controlled territory throughout Europe. There they, too, were murdered and entombed.

When the tide of war turned, officers in the German army ordered Ukrainian prisoners to excavate and obliterate all traces of the remains at Babi Yar. It took several weeks to complete the job. The bodies were incinerated; any bones that survived the flames were crushed and mixed with the earth to hide the evidence of the atrocities committed there.

God Had a Better Plan
The only snag was that God witnessed every sinful act committed against His people in that place. He made sure that detailed Nazi documents were preserved and that witnesses to the carnage came forward to describe what happened in 1941 and 1942.[9]

The remains of a synagogue we visited in Kishinev, Moldavia.

Some of the friends who visited Babi Yar with us had lost grandparents in that massacre. We bypassed the large national monument that had been erected in memory of the atrocity and went directly to the actual site where so many people lost their lives. The place was holy, sovereign and painful at the same time. In consideration and respect for our dear friends who had lost grandparents there, we did not launch any verbal prayers during our visit.

Several festivals later, in 1996, we embarked upon another strategic prayer assignment in Kishinev, Moldavia, the city where Joseph Rabinowitz established the first Messianic synagogue since the first century, nearly 100 years earlier (as we discussed in chapter 2). It would mark the culmination of our prophetic intercession efforts for that season of the Spirit, and it was to be one of our most significant prayer assignments.

LOCATING THE FIRST MESSIANIC CONGREGATION

Throughout our time in Kishinev, the heart of our prayer was that God would anoint the Messianic Jews of this generation with the same radicalism and fire evident in the lives and ministry of Paul, Peter and the other first-century Jewish leaders. We prayed that Jewish people in the Land of the North would come back into their full heritage just as Joseph Rabinowitz did. There is contagious devoted zeal that surfaces in certain Jewish followers of Yeshua (the Jewish name for Jesus) that is amazing.

Once again, we were involved in the intercessory and outreach aspects of each festival. Yet we spent a few days scouting around and just listening as God would lead us to key points of information and direct us to the exact place we were to launch our prophetic prayer.

Our first goal was to locate the place where Rabinowitz and the Israelites of the New Covenant had worshiped. That was difficult because nearly a century had passed. Many landmarks were destroyed during the pogroms against Jewish citizens of Kishinev in 1903 and 1905, and during the Nazi murder of 53,000 of the city's estimated 65,000 Jews in 1941.[10]

We found the original Jewish synagogue in Kishinev, but it was closed. Rabbi Richard Glickstein, a brother in Christ who was then leading a Messianic congregation in Moscow, found incredible favor on that prayer journey. After Glickstein talked with some people outside the synagogue, we were allowed to go in. As we walked around, we prayed for discernment and crucial information to guide our intercession in Kishinev. Before we left, we felt led to give a donation to the synagogue.

After praying and asking questions, we were ready for the next step in our journey: We had an address!

A Message in a Hole in the Wall

As we entered the neighborhood where we believed Rabinowitz's congregation may have met, we immediately noticed that most of the buildings were relatively new. We knew that meant that the original structures had been bombed during the war. Only one block of older buildings had somehow escaped destruction or extreme damage.

We parked the car in the old section. As we climbed out of the vehicle, we were all struck by the same sight: An old, 10-foot-high concrete wall stretched along for the full length of the block except for one place where a hole had been created. The buildings were perched on top of this foundation.

Our guide led us around to the back of the buildings where a number of doors led to apartments. We made our way to the door of the building we believed was built just above that hole in the foundation wall.

Since we looked like foreigners, we decided to play the part. It would have been unwise and virtually impossible to explain our prayer, so we entered what I call our "dumb, naive American tourist mode." (This comes under the "be wise as a serpent and gentle as a dove" principle.)

The building owners answered when we knocked on the door. Through our guide we said, "Hello, we are visitors from America. Could we tour your building?" For emphasis, we added that we had heard it had been used for something or another a long time ago.

The owners were very gracious, and they invited us in to examine their apartment building. We looked around, but we did not initially see anything that stood out. Then, just as we were about to leave, Fitzpatrick noticed a door leading to a stairwell to what appeared to be a cellar. There was something about that door that quickened his spirit. When the rest of us saw it, we knew we had to investigate further.

We had already established our identity as dumb American tourists, so we had nothing to lose. We asked, "Look! What's down there? This might be silly as can be, but can we go down in the cellar?"

The owners quickly nodded and motioned for us to freely explore the passageway. They must have been thinking, *Those crazy Americans! What will they want to see next?*

Fresh Oil of Anointing and Fresh Wine of God's Spirit

The stairway was nearly blocked by various items that had been stored for a long time. Nonetheless, we made our way down the stairs and turned right. When we entered the cellar, we looked at each other, amazed. We could see daylight streaming into the room through the hole in the wall we had seen from the street. Old bottles of wine, still packed in their cases, were stacked on a pallet and empty bottles of olive oil were scattered about on the shelves in the room.

The prophetic symbolism of the scene was almost overwhelming. Immediately we knew this was the place where we would complete our assignment and release "fresh oil of the anointing" and "fresh wine of God's Spirit" into the Jewish people.

Redigging the Wells, Just like Isaac

Just as Isaac had his men redig the wells of his father, Abraham (see Gen. 26); there is a spiritual concept of redigging the ancient wells of the anointing of those who walked with God in earlier generations, even in the face of opposition.[11] Therefore, it was part of our assignment to issue a prophetic on-site prayer to release God's high anointing on His ancient people and to urge them to escape the old walls that were closing in upon them. We were to call forth the apostolic grace of church planting that had originated and rested on that location. We were to call forth the new wine and the fresh oil of the Holy Spirit. (Glickstein ended up going all over the former Soviet states raising up numerous Messianic synagogues).

This is why the hole in the wall is significant. It was time for God's ancient covenant people to return to their land of promise from the land of captivity with the help of the Gentiles who received the New Covenant through the Jewish people. Perhaps it also indicated there was an opening to pray.

The Lord had led us to the exact place where He birthed the first Messianic Jewish congregation nearly a century earlier. He took us to their very foundations, to a place still containing prophetic signs of empty olive oil bottles and old wine bottles.

By that time we knew the research portion of our journey was over. We had the information we needed, but we agreed that we were not to pray overtly in this couple's basement. After thanking our bewildered hosts for their hospitality, we returned to the front of the building where the hole breached the old wall. We were in total agreement that this was the spot where the Lord wanted us to pray. Together we released the prayer that we had come to deliver to the city of Kishinev. Out of death and decay would arise a new anointing and fiery zeal to restore the Jews of the diaspora to the God of Israel and to their long-awaited Messiah, Yeshua.

TRAVELING IN ISRAEL WITH THE CALEB COMPANY

Another transformation began to take place after the fall of Communism. It is still transforming Israel and highlighting the importance of Russian Jews making aliyah. I discovered this phenomenon in a personal and painful way when Fitzpatrick and I went on a prayer journey to Israel with a group called the Caleb Company.

Dr. Don Finto, the former senior pastor at Belmont Church, in Nashville, Tennessee, and author of *Your People Shall Be My People*, had launched the ministry to build upon supernatural favor he had experienced in developing networks and friendships among Messianic leaders of various backgrounds. Finto named the ministry after Caleb who, according to the book of Numbers, had a "different spirit." He was a man anointed to look into the Promised Land and take the land without fear of enemies or obstacles.[12]

Five Caleb Company board members, including Fitzpatrick and me, traveled to Israel with Finto. We wanted to discover God's heart for the nation and the Jewish people.

Finto hoped we would grow in our understanding of the Jewish people. He also wanted us to meet with key government and Messianic community leaders from across the promised land.

With the Pain Came an Astounding Word

My painful adventure began during a stopover in a remote area north of Tel Aviv. That night I had a peculiar dream in which I was stabbed. The pain of the wound was so agonizing that I woke to find myself tangled up in blankets, and my body literally wracked with pain! I did not know whether the attack was physical or spiritual in nature, so I started repenting of anything and everything I had ever done wrong (and a million things I have not done). It was 2 A.M., and nothing seemed to alleviate the anguish.

Finally I decided to get help. But I was in so much pain that I could not stand up. I rolled off of the bed, hitting the floor with a thud. I was in excruciating pain, but eventually, I was able to crawl out of my room into the Kibbutzim where we were staying. Then I managed to pound on the door of Finto's room—it was the middle of the night! When he opened the door, he had to look down to figure out who was crazy enough to wake him up at that hour. He immediately contacted our guide and fellow intercessor, Rabbi Avner Boskey, because he spoke fluent Hebrew. They rushed me to a nearby hospital.

I do not remember much of what happened next. My mind was too fuzzy. I later learned that the hospital staff ran a series of tests and gave me powerful painkillers, which had little apparent effect. The pain gradually lifted, but the doctor, who believed I was suffering from kidney stones, gave me more medication, "just in case."

I was ordered to stay in the hospital to recuperate, even though I could now recognize my surroundings. When I met my doctor, I was surprised to discover he was a *Russian* Jew. He was so Russian that he could only speak Russian, not Hebrew. I thought to myself, *Well, this is interesting. I have been praying for the release of the Russian Jews, and here I am at the absolute mercy of a Russian Jewish doctor in Israel.*

God Begins to Speak

After I was released, our Caleb Company traveled to a villa (a prayer house) located outside the old walls of Jerusalem. We could see the city from where we stayed. We had barely settled in when the excruciating pain hit me again. Wanting to tough it out, I took the medicine prescribed by my Russian Jewish doctor.

Despite the painkillers, I could not sleep. That was alright, because from my window I was able to watch an incredibly beautiful snowfall upon Jerusalem. In the end, toughing it out did not work. I again had to be taken to a doctor. This time I was checked into Hadassah Hospital. (Hadassah is the feminine Hebrew word for myrtle tree. It is also the Hebrew name of Esther, the queen who, in the Old Testament, stood up for her Jewish people.)

When I arrived at the hospital, I was in agonizing pain. Yet, at the same time, the Lord was speaking to me. He communicated in dreams, visions and revelations about a variety of issues. He revealed specific plots of the enemy—such as where bombs were planted on the West Bank.

The Revelations Came to Pass

I knew these revelations were not the by-product of medication. My prayer partners and I would pray through each point God had raised. We would cry out for intervention until we received assurances from the Lord that breakthrough had been made. Invariably, each event would show up on the front page of the newspaper the next day.

One day we read in the paper that the snow that had fallen in the night had so disrupted traffic that officials had called off school. Israeli security forces subsequently found a bomb-making plant in the West Bank—it was in the exact location God had revealed to me. The paper surmised that the snow had stopped traffic and foiled the plans of the terrorists "for no known reason." But we knew why.

Once again, I had Russian Jewish doctors attend me during my hospital stay. They prescribed more pain pills and more tests. I will never forget the way one of the Messianic Jewish leaders from Jerusalem sat with me the entire day and selflessly served me.

Disappearing Pain Befuddles Russian Doctors

My Russian-speaking doctors were perplexed with me because on the one hand, their X ray and sonogram exams showed clear evidence that I had been suffering from kidney stones. On the other hand, a second round of tests failed to find anything and all of my pain simply disappeared. It appears that the Lord simply dissolved it.

I find it significant that at two separate hospitals in Israel, I had Russian Jewish doctors treating me. The migration from Russia is beginning to transform Israel. Everywhere we went, we found Russian Jews and heard the Russian language spoken. *God is calling His people out of the Land of the North in unprecedented numbers!*

God spoke through Zechariah the prophet and said, "I will make Jerusalem a heavy stone" (see Zech. 12:3). My experience during the Caleb Company's tour of Israel was a warning. I feel that I tasted the reality of the agony and pain mixed with the blessings that come to anyone who dares to identify with the suffering our Messiah endured for us.

God's Purpose Comes Through Redemptive Identification

The Lord used the trip as a tool of redemptive identification to help me relate to the pain of the Jewish people and to show me the kind of agonizing prayer needed to bring forth the fullness of God's purposes among the Jewish people.

In prophetic retrospect, it is obvious that the "wealth" God is returning to Israel is in the form of Russian Jewish medical doctors, rocket engineers, physicists, musicians, writers, chemists and numerous other highly skilled people.

Teachers of Bible prophecy have speculated for years about various end-time scenarios, but I find it quite amazing that virtually no one fully foresaw the radical changes in Russia preceding the end of the second millennium.

Could it be that the biblical predictions of conflict between God and Magog (understood to be the region of the former Soviet Union) might be triggered by divinely engineered jealousy? Will Israel become so Russian due to a potential population of 3 million Russian Jews that the Land of the North will move to supposedly "reclaim its own"? Will jealousy be the "hook" God places in the jaw of Israel's adversary to the north to trigger the ill-fated invasion written about in the book of Revelation that is destined to end in the Battle of Armageddon?[13]

PART III

A PROPHETIC PROCLAMATION—
GAZING INTO THE FUTURE

CHAPTER 7

TAKING THE PULSE OF GOD AND HIS PEOPLE

But when He, the Spirit of truth, comes, He will guide you into all the truth;
for He will not speak on His own initiative, but whatever He hears,
He will speak; and He will disclose to you what is to come.

JOHN 16:13

God is pleased when men and women take the time to understand the issues of the times. He is delighted when we seek to understand the ways He deals with us. The first book of Chronicles said the sons of Issachar were "men who understood the times, with knowledge of what Israel should do" (1 Chron. 12:32). This kind of knowledge can only come from God. We are a people who must learn to discern the times in which we live and glean from the lessons of past generations. *May the sons of Issachar arise for this generation!*

The more critical the times, the more important is our need to seek God for understanding, knowledge and direction. I call this "taking the pulse of God," much as a nurse takes a patient's pulse to determine the heart rate of a person. What is beating God's heart? What is He saying through His written Word? What is He revealing through the voice of the Holy Spirit? What is He doing among men right now? What part are we to play in His plan?

Sometimes God uses seemingly insignificant events in seemingly insignificant locations to give advance warning or prophetic indications of what is coming on a global or generational scale. For example, God used ordinary people tucked away in an insignificant manger in Bethlehem to transform the world.

FINDING REDEMPTION IN AUSTRIA

In 1996, David Fitzpatrick, a group of friends and I took another missions trip. This time we went to the small city of Wiener Neustadt, south of Vienna, Austria. We were there to lead a prophetic conference. Fitzpatrick and his family had just completed a divine assignment to assist the Avner Boskey family and other leaders of new Messianic congregations in Saint Petersburg and Moscow, Russia. They were ready to return to the United States. When I called Fitzpatrick about the Austria conference, he said the Lord impressed upon him that he *had* to come. Something special was going to happen. So we made arrangements to rendezvous in Vienna.

A team of German leaders and several intercessory and prophetic friends joined us for this gathering. Rich and Gale Harris, the founders of Living Word Ministries International and the senior ministers of The Front Range S.O.S. (a Denver, Colorado-based congregation and school of the Spirit) also came. The Harrises went with Michal Ann and me on the first prayer tour we led to Israel with Rabbi Boskey of Final Frontier Ministries. They were apprehended by the Holy Spirit on that trip and stayed in touch with us afterward. It was a joy to have them with us for the conference in Austria, but there was much more going on than any of us anticipated.

A wonderful interdenominational church, founded by Pastor Helmuth and Uli Eiwen in Wiener Neustadt, sponsored the conference. Helmuth was originally a Lutheran pastor, but he felt led to establish a pioneer work called the Ichthys Church. There seemed to be a hindrance in the city that stymied every effort to bring life to the area. The Eiwens and their prayer group had been seeking God for the answer to the questions, What is wrong with this city? What are the hindrances standing in our way, keeping us from making an impact for the gospel?

The First Vision: A Small Book Revealed

After seeking the Lord, Uli received several open-eyed revelatory visions. In the first one, she saw a small book surrounded by darkness. A bright light suddenly illuminated the book and Uli recognized a part of the old city wall in Wiener Neustadt. The next day they found the old section of the wall—along with something else they never expected. Gail Harris has written a book about the Eiwens' prophetic journey titled *Reconciliation*. In it she recounts:

> There they found that six Jewish tombstones had been affixed to the wall as a monument. Next to them was written an inscription: "These tombstones came from a Jewish cemetery in Wiener Neustadt that was closed in 1496."[1]

The Eiwens examined the historical record to see what happened 500 years earlier. They discovered that Wiener Neustadt was home to the second largest community of Jews in Austria. Unfortunately, that beautiful locale was also the favorite city of Emperor Maximilian I, a member of the Hapsburg dynasty and the ruler of what was called The Holy Roman Empire. Three years after he ascended to the throne, the 34-year-old monarch issued a devastating decree that remained in force for 300 years:

> All Jews from Wiener Neustadt must leave the city and for all time and eternity they may not come back.[2]

This Royal Decree was actually a demonic curse that, within 150 years, brought cultural and financial destruction to the entire city. However, the gates of Wiener Neustadt reopened to Jewish people around 1900. By the 1930s, 1,200 Jewish citizens lived in the city, the fourth largest Jewish community in Austria. Then the Nazis annexed Austria in the Anschluss of 1938.

The Eiwens discovered, to their horror, that many of Wiener Neustadt's Jewish children had been separated from their parents and sent away. Later, the older Jewish citizens had been shipped off to concentration camps where most of them died. Therefore, any survivors from the Jewish community in Wiener Neustadt were most likely children during the war. The Eiwens led the leadership of Ichthys Church in repentant prayer for the sins of the past, but somehow they sensed that something more, something *personal* and *public* had to be done.

The Second Vision: A Tree of Healing

Uli received another vision in which she saw a young tree with ancient roots on the city wall in front of the gravestones. The Lord called it a Tree of Healing, and compared it to the Body of Christ. He said that it would bring healing to its ancient roots—the city of Wiener Neustadt and to the Jews who suffered so much in that place.

After receiving a prophetic word from a visiting American minister concerning delegations of Jews from all over the world coming to Wiener Neustadt, the Eiwens felt they knew what they had to do. They set out to find Jewish survivors of the Holocaust who originally lived in their city. It was an impossible task, but God intervened to give them the name of a Jewish man living in Israel. He was the son of the last head rabbi of Wiener Neustadt, who had died at the hands of the Nazis.

The Eiwens traveled to Israel to meet this man and tell him what God said they must do. He, in turn, helped them contact 25 other Jewish survivors from Wiener Neustadt. Eventually, almost the entire church congregation in Wiener Neustadt went to Israel, where they met in Haifa with a group of survivors!

Holocaust Survivors Return to "Beachhead"

Three groups of Jewish Holocaust survivors returned to Wiener Neustadt from Israel and other parts of the world *at the church's expense!* Each time, the Eiwens and their church congregation asked forgiveness for the wrongs done during World War II. A supernatural spirit of reconciliation brought healing and close relationships that continue to this day. This is monumental. *Yes, the spots and the stains in the Church's garment shall be cleansed!*

In the summer of 1995, my oldest son, Justin, and I visited the Eiwens at their home in Wiener Neustadt. We were having breakfast one morning when I began to pray for them. Suddenly, in a vision, I saw the date, June 6, appear across Helmuth's forehead! They told me about a prophetic word they had received the year before that said, "You are people who pray for one specific city, and this city will be a *beachhead*."[3]

Shortly after our breakfast together, the Eiwens were in England and they received a prophetic reminder that Allied troops had established a *beachhead* and turned the tide of World War II at Normandy on *June 6*, 1944. The Eiwens knew that another army, an army of God, was destined to establish a spiritual beachhead in Wiener Neustadt: first in the natural, and then in the spiritual.

On June 6, 1996—six years after the Eiwens established Ichthys Church and 500 years after Maximilian I banned the Jewish people from the city of Wiener Neustadt—the third group of Jewish Holocaust survivors returned to the city. They heard Helmuth Eiwen ask them, "Please forgive us . . ." Since that group included more than 10 Jewish men, a Sabbath service was held at the request of the son of the Wiener Neustadt's last Jewish rabbi before the Nazis came.

Breakthrough Comes at Menorah Service

The Holocaust survivors and their Gentile sponsors gathered in front of the memorial in the old wall of the city. Then the son of the rabbi, now an elderly grandfather, uttered ancient prayers from God's Word. He and his grandson blew out the candles of a silver menorah brought from Israel for the service. Then the Jewish visitors gave the menorah to the Eiwens as a memorial gift. Gail Harris described what happened after the service:

> After the Sabbath service, a Sabbath meal was held in the hotel. An inexplicable joy suddenly broke through. They couldn't describe it—it was like an explosion. It began with singing. The men stood up and began to dance with one another. The windows were wide open because it was so hot, and others could hear the singing all over the city. These were the sounds of a people who had been set free. They never would have imagined even being able to laugh in this city. One of the wives said to Uli, "I have NEVER seen my husband dance!"[4]

Breakthrough came when Jews and Gentiles lit the candles of the menorah. They came together at the place where the tombstones of the disenfranchised Jews signified their rejection by men through the decree of Maximilian I and marked the tragic betrayal and death of the Jews of Wiener Neustadt. Like Aaron of old had done, a line was drawn in the sand. The death plague was checked and life began (see Num. 16:44-49).

The prophetic action of relighting the candles representative of the light of Jehovah in the ancient Holy Place of the Tabernacles and the Temple of Solomon was a picture of how Gentiles offer again the light we received through Jewish people. I am speaking, of course, of the light of the Messiah, who entered the world and redeemed all men as the ancient Scriptures said He would. What happened in Wiener Neustadt was a landmark act of identificational repentance reminiscent of the restoration Paul described in Romans 11.

The wall in Weiner Neustadt, Austria, which was the sight of reconciliation gatherings between Jewish people and Christians.

Extending Restoration Beyond the Walls of the Church

Unique to the gathering in Wiener Neustadt was how it affected more than just the people inside of a church building or the relatively small number of Jewish Holocaust survivors who traveled from Israel. The entire city felt the impact and was deeply involved in this reconciliation and repentance. At the invitation of the mayor, some of the Jewish visitors spoke to students at the local high school. They described what happened to them and their families during the Holocaust—this attracted wide media exposure. In another spin-off from the gathering, a student exchange program was established between the school in Wiener Neustadt and a high school in Bat Yam, near Tel Aviv, Israel. This will influence generations to come.

We perceived that there was a "governmental mantle" imparted to Helmut and Uli Eiwen to not only *bring* the reconciliation of God to Jewish people and Gentiles, but also to *take it* to secular institutions and governments. Three months after the Sabbath service took place in front of the old wall in Wiener Neustadt, the Eiwens brought the silver menorah with them to Nashville, Tennessee, at the invitation of Fitzpatrick and members of our prayer team.

BLOWING THE TRUMPET IN NASHVILLE

I was still living in Kansas City, Missouri, at the time, but was deeply involved in prayer for Israel and for the Jewish people who still resided in the Land of the North. Don Finto, Fitzpatrick, a number of other intercessors and I sensed there was a strong redemptive gift of God upon the city of Nashville and a *place of a stewardship from the Lord* for that city to "blow a trumpet" for Israel. There were many people in Nashville who had done much on behalf of Israel, and our prayer was to have a spiritual "candlestick" (similar to the "lampstand" seen in Revelation 1:12) planted in Nashville on behalf of Israel. I share this not to elevate Nashville, but to reveal the spiritual principles involved in our prophetic prayer journey.

Fitzpatrick brought the Eiwens to Nashville on February 13, 1997, for a historic prayer convocation at Finto's Belmont Church. My wife and I flew from Kansas City to attend the event. When the Eiwens spoke—God began to move. We lit the menorah candle and asked the Lord to give us, as representatives of the city, a heavenly lamp stand on behalf of Israel.

Music City Becomes Worship City

During the service, the Lord spoke to me. I even wrote His words in my Bible: "You were born for this city, and this city was born for you." It was a spiritual ambush. My wife and I had come to support this prophetic act, but the Lord had bigger plans. He snared us into moving to Music City. The following June, my family and I moved to Nashville. We reestablished our ministry base in what I have come to call "Worship City USA." Nashville now also hosts a prayer watch for Israel and Jewish people around the world.

At that time Finto was emerging as a spiritual father and friend to Messianic Jews all over Israel. He became so involved with this God-given mandate that he turned the pastorate of Belmont, a 4,000-member Spirit-filled church, over to one of his associates. To facilitate his new outreach, Finto launched Caleb Company, a ministry introduced in chapter 6.

Passing the Baton

As this group of intercessors with a heart for Jewish people assembled in Nashville, it became clear to us that what God began in the Land of the North was being exported by the Holy Spirit to other cities and nations. If the Second Great Exodus could be compared to a marathon relay, then we were being handed a baton, only it was obvious there would be more than one baton to pass on.

With the lighting of the menorah, what had started in Wiener Neustadt, Austria, had come to Nashville, Tennessee. In turn, we prayed at a conference mentioned at the beginning of this book in Sunderland, England, where God lit a candle of anointing and authority to reconcile Gentiles and Jews. This ancient city on the North Sea was the historical shipbuilding center of the British Empire during the era of wooden ships, and in recent years, a stream of renewal has broken out in the church pastored by Ken and Lois Gott.

In a way, we were permitted by the Lord to help pass batons on from Austria and the Land of the North. We handed them off in England and Western Europe. In Sunderland the Holy Spirit linked together the revelations on Israel and the Land of the North, which He had given to me and to Cindy Jacobs. All of this culminated in December of 1999 at The World Congress on Intercession mentioned in the opening of this book. The Congress released a major prophetic statement to the Church. It clearly warned of a demonic strategy to "precipitate another holocaust" and urged the Church to pray for all Jewish people—especially those living in the Land of the North.[5]

It was as if a time bomb had gone off in the spirit as Cindy Jacobs, Chuck Pierce and I led prayers for Russia and God's purposes among the Jewish people. That night the Israel Prayer Watch was launched in Nashville. *Truly, the Lord was orchestrating something mighty!*

SUPPORT FOR JEWISH PEOPLE GROWS

God was moving others to act on behalf of Jewish people, too. The World Prayer Center in Colorado Springs, Colorado, had set up a prayer effort they called the 10/40 Window, (targeting so-called Third World nations in the 1990s. For the years 2000 to 2005, that effort has been expanded to a 40/70 Window, which includes all of Europe and the former Soviet Union. Intercessors are encouraged to pray for the gospel of Jesus Christ to come forth, for closed hearts to become opened and for demonic powers to be thwarted. Prayer walks and other strategic acts of intercession will proceed to build on what has already been offered up to the Lord. Intercessors are also exhorted to call forth God's purposes among the Jewish people in the Land of the North!

Perhaps the greatest short-term impact of this new prophetic direction came when members of the Spiritual Warfare Network (now called the Strategic Prayer Network) consulted with Messianic leaders and other Church leaders to draft a historic statement of repentance to the Jewish people in America and the nations of the world.

On January 13, 2000, members of the Spiritual Warfare Network presented a wreath and a signed copy of this statement to representatives of the National Holocaust Museum in Washington, D.C. At the presentation, after the statement was read, the intercessors ended up on the floor repenting and weeping before God.

I can think of no better way to portray what we believe to be the pulse of God's heart in this generation than to reproduce this statement of repentance and reconciliation in its complete and unedited form:

Statement of Repentance to the Jewish People in America and the Nations of the World

Dear Respected Friends in the Jewish Community who share in our common faith in the G-d of Abraham, Isaac and Jacob,

Something is happening in our generation that we deem to be motivated by the Almighty. People of different ethnic backgrounds and national origins are acknowledging the sins of past generations against each other in a desire for reconciliation and peace. The sons and daughters of former slave traders are taking upon themselves the sins of their forebears and confessing these sins to the sons and daughters of former slaves. You may be aware that a "Reconciliation Walk" was recently taken between Europe and Jerusalem by a group of Christians who were confessing the sins of the devastations of the Crusades.

We know that the Jewish people throughout the centuries have borne the greatest discrimination, the worst persecution and the most barbaric atrocities of all. We, too, have read the histories. We are aware that much of this has been done by Christians or by those who called themselves Christians, sometimes while calling upon the name of Christ.

This is a grotesque misrepresentation of the one who is called the Prince of Peace and who called us to love and to worship our Heavenly Father and to love our neighbor as ourselves. Though the Scriptures we call the New Testament have exhorted us to love, respect and exercise mercy towards you, the ancient people of G-d, and G-d's chosen people to this day, we and our forefathers in the Christian faith have rebelled against that command and have acted out of fear, prejudice, hatred and jealousy. Those who have not so acted have acquiesced by their silence during the times of crusades, pogrom and finally in the terrifying holocaust.

Nor are we Christian believers in the United States without our own share in this guilt. Not only are many of us descended from the perpetrators of these crimes, but our forefathers stood by without registering complaint when, in the years of the reign of horror in Europe, Jewish refugees were turned away from our shores. Our forefathers turned their eyes away from the death plight of the European Jewish community. Even in recent years, some in the Christian community have often stood in apathy as synagogues have been torched, cemeteries desecrated and Jewish homes and businesses vandalized.

We grieve over these crimes against you, our Jewish brothers and sisters, and in the spirit of Daniel, who confessed the sins of former generations, we confess these horrors as sins and renounce them. We understand from our reading of the Prophet Zechariah that a time will yet come when the whole world turns against Israel. Should such a thing come to pass, many of us want to be numbered with those few Gentile Christians through the centuries who have risked their lives to protect you. **We commit ourselves to standing with you in the strength of G-d, whatever the cost.[6]**

Acts of Reconciliation in Canada

Our brothers and sisters in Christ in Canada have taken the commitment to stand with the Jewish people even a step further. On November 5, 2000, a historic gathering convened in Ottawa. Participants held a time of repentance and reconciliation with survivors of the ship *Saint Louis*.

Three hundred believers representing the Church came together in humility to ask for forgiveness for the shameful deed. In May 1939, a ship with 900 Jewish men, women and children aboard was turned away from Canadian shores. Among those who spoke on behalf of the Canadian Church were David Mainse, host of the "100 Huntley Street" television show; Archbishop

Gervais, representing the Canadian Council of Bishops; and Doug Blair (nephew of the former deputy immigration minister, Fred Blair). Ken Hall from West Ottawa Christian Community chaired the gathering. Here is the document they released:

DECLARATION FROM THE CHURCH IN CANADA

We, as a body of concerned Christians representing the many streams of the Church in Canada, humbly make this Declaration to the survivors of the Holocaust and the *Saint Louis* ship. In the merciful prompting of God, we have been on a long prayerful journey of several years to bring us to this historic occasion. Our sincere expressions today are the fruit of much travel, numerous consultations, sacrificial giving and active involvement of thousands of Christians across Canada.

We express our deep sorrow and genuine repentance for the sins of our forefathers and the subsequent atrocities you have personally suffered. We are grieved that in May 1939, Canada rejected the *St. Louis* ship, carrying over 900 Jewish men, women and children, looking for a place of refuge from the Nazi regime in Europe.

We are shamed by the memory of Canada not honouring the commitment to bring 1000 Jewish children from a refugee camp in France to our shores in November, 1942.

We admit that these two deplorable episodes were the result of strong anti-Semitic sentiment within Canada. The passive silence of the Canadian Church supported the Government's tragic policies and decisions.

We identify with the sins of the past regarding the Holocaust and we ask the forgiveness of you and all Jewish people. We endorse the pledge of our Prime

Minister, the Honourable Jean Chretien, during his April 2000 visit to Yad Vashem:

> As Prime Minister of Canada, I pledge to you that Canada will take a leading role to ensure that such atrocities never happen again.

- We warmly express our love to you and to all Jewish people in Israel and in the global Diaspora.
- We denounce any unbiblical beliefs within the Church that result in harmful attitudes and actions toward the Jewish people.
- We commit to stand with the Jewish people for righteousness and justice in all nations.
- We pledge to continue our intercession for Jewish people by heeding King David's exhortation in Psalm 122:

> Pray for the peace of Jerusalem: "May they prosper who love you. May peace be within your walls, and prosperity within your palaces." For the sake of my brothers and my friends, I will now say, "May peace be within you." For the sake of the house of the Lord our God, I will seek your good.

November 5, 2000   Ottawa-Hull, Canada

These changes are wonderful! But more must happen. I sense a shift occurring in the heart of the Body of Christ. In taking the pulse of God and His people, I feel a beat pulsating with the rhythm of God's heart in the Body of Christ. Change is coming. Change must come. Change is on the way!

CHAPTER 8

THE MORDECAI CALLING: A GAZE INTO THE FUTURE

For if you remain silent at this time, relief and deliverance will arise for the Jews from another place and you and your father's house will perish. And who knows whether you have not attained royalty for such a time as this?

ESTHER 4:14

There is an ancient, malevolent spirit plaguing our planet. It is unmoved, unimpressed and unafraid of human intellectual enlightenment. It has no regard for human reason, logic, good intentions or mere religious pursuits. It is the dark spirit of anti-Semitism—or what may be called "the spirit of Haman," named after the man who plotted to exterminate the Jewish people in the days of King Artaxerxes of Persia (see the book of Esther).

As Christians we have a dangerous tendency to commit to the myth bin or to the pleasant childhood Bible story corner Bible narratives such as the story of Esther, Mordecai and Haman. God never gave us permission to do this. The Bible still declares, "All Scripture is inspired by God and profitable for teaching, for reproof, for correction, for training in righteousness."[1]

This ancient spirit of genocide still lives. It yields only to the power of God, and that power can only be released by a people who pray, fast and put themselves at risk for the sake of His ancient Covenant People, the Jews.

A DIVINE APPOINTMENT
IN BERLIN

The reality of this age-old nemesis of the Jews was driven further home to me in 1992, during one of my first trips to the central European nations right after the fall of Communism. After I ministered in the nations formerly known as Yugoslavia and Czechoslovakia, I rode a train from Prague in the Czech Republic to Berlin, Germany. I traveled alone because I wanted to seek the Lord. Being a "Goll" of German descent, for years I have carried a heart for the German-speaking world, desiring that the wrongs of the past would be righted.

I took advantage of the free time on the train to read Dr. David Yonggi Cho's book, *Daniel: Insight on the Life and Dreams of the Prophet from Babylon.*[2] The book cover featured a striking photograph of a beastlike character. I was intrigued by this mosaic depicting the ancient Isthar Gate of Babylon and mused on what it meant. I even pondered why I was reading this book at this time.

Cho penned a remarkable phrase in the text: "In order to make a nation stand upright, the evil prince which is behind the nation must be driven away through prayer. The demon which seeks to steal and kill an individual or a family must also be bound in prayer."[3] The principles revealed in this book flowed right into the revelations presented in the second book I read on that long train trip, *Engaging the Enemy: How to Fight and Defeat Territorial Spirits*, by Dr. C. Peter Wagner.[4]

Guided by the Holy Spirit

Although I had previously visited Germany, I only knew a few phrases in German. I had never been to Berlin. I did not even know where to get off the train or how to find lodging. But my guide, the Holy Spirit, knew the layout of the land quite well.

My train trip ended at the Berlin Wall.[5] I made it to a hotel and did not leave my room for nearly three days. After being holed up spending time in prayer, I sensed God releasing me to walk through the city to pray. That was when I literally stumbled across the Pergamon Museum, a place I did not know existed. (Pergamon can also be called Pergamum.)

Finding "The Seat of Satan"

In the book of Revelation, the Spirit said to the angel of the Church of Pergamum, "I know where you dwell, *where Satan's throne is*; and you hold fast My name, and did not deny My faith even in the days of Antipas, My witness, My faithful one, who was killed among you, *where Satan dwells*."[6]

As far as I know, this is the only mention in the Scriptures of a physical site where Satan's throne could be found. Pergamum was also called the place where the adversary *dwelled* or lived. It was not surprising to learn that in the original Greek, *pergamum* literally means "fortified, fortress, or castle."[7]

I went into the museum and was shocked to find myself staring at the exact beastlike idol pictured on the front of Cho's book! Only this was the *original, the real thing*. How could it be? Let me unfold a bit of what I learned on that journey.

Sometime between 1878 and 1886 (close to the time Joseph Rabinowitz met the Messiah and took the good news from the Middle East back to his home in Eastern Europe), German engineer and archaeologist Karl Humann excavated the ruins of Pergamum in what is now Turkey. Most of what is called the Great Altar of Zeus was removed from Pergamum and shipped to Germany's Berlin Museum.[8] The stone sections of the Altar of Zeus remained in storage until they were reconstructed stone by stone. The completed work is called the Pergamum Altar.

The Pergamon Museum also contains Athena's Temple and a model of ancient Babylon's Ishtar Gate and Processional Way. They represent with chilling power the ancient enemy of Israel and the God of Israel. Here, right in front of my eyes, were the original artifacts from ancient Babylon.

After I had read about Daniel, the prophet to Babylon, in Cho's book, I entered this reconstructed pagan shrine the Bible describes as "the seat of Satan." To put this in context, the day I stepped into the reassembled Altar of Zeus in Berlin, the children of Israel were again in captivity, but this time in the Land of the North. They had reached the end of another 70-year period (compare Dan. 9:1-19 with Jer. 25:11 and 29:10) and another conquering nation was in turmoil after touching the "apple of God's eye." Not only did the Jewish people begin their journey homeward in Daniel's day at the end of 70 years—but the walls of Soviet Communism also came tumbling down at exactly the 70-year mark of their origins! And there I was, staring at the restored ruins of the time that Daniel spoke about. I wanted to maximize this once-in-a-lifetime "divine appointment."

I felt it was time to intercede quietly in the Spirit. I softly prayed that the same God who had enlightened Daniel would now enlighten me. As I waited upon God, the proverbial light began to go on. Massive pieces of a jigsaw puzzle started to fall into place. I was beginning to understand what God had orchestrated.

The most amazing aspect of my "prayer journey" to the Pergamon Museum was the experience of walking into a building and suddenly being confronted by the very pagan deity—the genuine original image—that I saw pictured on the front of Cho's book on Babylon and Daniel's prophecies. This was the actual graven idol that men bowed to and worshiped in Pergamum when John received the warning in the book of Revelation!

Spiritual Roots of Anti-Semitism
I pondered the possibilities. Was there a connection to the spirit of anti-Semitism having a base of operation and this occultic high place being reestablished? Could this be one of the power points that was used to empower Hitler's reign of terror? I mused. I listened. I learned. But please understand, whenever

there is a major threat, God also counters it with an assault in His kingdom. Wherever there is conflict, it is because there is great purpose. God always has a plan and He always reveals it to His servants the prophets (see Amos 3:7).

This brooding antichrist, anti-Semitic spirit is, and has been, raising its ugly head all around the world—especially in Russia, the Balkans and other nations, as it has in the past.

A New Anti-Semitic Wave

What do we see when we gaze into the future? Most of the time, to view the future accurately, we must have a proper reading of yesterday's headlines and an accurate pulse on today. Where are we now? What are the current conditions in the Land of the North and the nations of the world? Is the spirit of anti-Semitism at work now? Are there any signs to read to give us some clues?

As pressures began to mount in Russia, Rabbi Richard Glickstein, who had been working with Messianic congregations in Moscow, moved to the West. Anti-Semitism has recently risen with a vengeance. Firebombings, persecution and violence have occurred on a regular basis. Even the number of Jewish people allowed to receive visas to immigrate to Israel has now been legally reduced. What does all this mean?

As an American and a Jew, Glickstein could have become a target of harassment. A growing number of Russians have begun to show greater animosity toward Westerners and to blame the United States for their economic woes. Glickstein moved his family from Moscow to Germany where he worked with a pocket of Russian Jews. Then he relocated to Finland so he could be postured to help the growing number of Russian-speaking Jewish people who want to leave the former Soviet states. Like pieces on a chessboard, modern-day Mordecais are being positioned for what is about to come—the Second Great Exodus! In Esther, Mordecai had warned the Queen about Haman's plot against the Jews (see Esther 3—4).

Jews Targeted Around the World

In Russia, anti-Semitic terrorists have vandalized Jewish synagogues and cultural centers and attempted to assassinate
leading Jewish figures. Russian Jewish leaders claim that an
"increasing number of [Russian] political figures . . . have with
impunity issued anti-Semitic statements as part of their effort to
win popular support."[9]

Austria, the nation that gave us some of the great com-
posers, philosophers and artists, also produced Adolf Hitler and
the Nazi movement. In 2000, a far-right political party headed
by alleged Nazi-sympathizer, Joerg Haider, was allowed to join
the ruling coalition of the Austrian government. It is said that
the move sent shock waves throughout Europe. The Jewish people in both Austria and neighboring Hungary feel the growing
threat of anti-Semitism once again breathing down their necks.
At this writing, the ruling party in Hungary's capital, Budapest,
is headed by Laszlo Kover. Rabbi David Levine calls Kover "bla-
tantly anti-Semitic."[10]

Even the United States has felt the pangs of growing anti-
Semitic violence. On the Saturday before Palm Sunday 1999, three
of the five Jewish synagogues in Sacramento, California, were firebombed. Rick Stivers, who also had moved to Moscow with his
family to get God's heart for the Russian Jews, at one point visited one of the burned-out synagogues while fire marshals, police
and the FBI were still conducting their investigations. He collect-
ed pieces of the burned synagogues. He and his wife, Annie, have
them in their home and use them as a prayer reminder to cry out
to the Lord on behalf of the Jewish people. Stivers commented: "I
wondered if, in the last 50 years, there had been any other city in
the world that had seen three synagogues torched in one day."[11]

Problems Mount in Russia and Germany

Meanwhile, social, economic and spiritual conditions in the former USSR and united Germany continue to deteriorate. On the

verge of collapse, Russia's outdated and inadequate medical system cannot keep pace with a dramatic increase of infectious diseases. A report in the *New York Times* stated:

> Russia's political turmoil, its economic crisis and its new freedoms have been accompanied by a wave of old diseases. Tuberculosis is flooding the country, producing what some authorities are calling the world's largest outbreak of the drug-resistant variety, one of medicine's most ominous problems.
>
> Rates of other infections, including hepatitis, syphilis and AIDS, are skyrocketing. An epidemic of diphtheria swept through in the mid-1990s. Reports of smaller, regional outbreaks of encephalitis, typhoid fever, malaria, polio, pneumonia and influenza pepper the nightly news....
>
> Specialists worry that if the rising rates of infectious diseases in Russia continue unabated, the country itself may turn into an epidemiologic pump, sending infectious diseases into the rest of the world.[12]

The former Soviet states have suffered devastating crop losses in recent years. In 1988, Russian farmers brought in their worst harvest in 40 years, forcing the nation to turn to the outside world for help. Things have only gone downhill since then. Experts in the U.S. Agriculture Department said in the year 2000 that Russia's chronic problems in producing animal feed will continue into 2001. Most observers believe it will go on far longer than that because of the combination of Russia's fiscal calamity, poor agricultural performance and hardening world attitudes toward a nation that continues to wage war in outlying provinces such as Chechnya.[13]

Germany faces problems trying to reunite its people after decades of separation and deprivation due to the imposition of

Communism on half of its population. The "haves" are doing their best to accommodate the "have-nots." But what does the future hold? Questions linger on the horizon. This is why we must get God's heart at this crucial hour!

Historically, people who face a crisis seek out a scapegoat. One group of people has been singled out as the world's favorite scapegoat for centuries: the Jewish people. Once again, it appears that God's timing in calling His Covenant People to aliyah is perfectly timed and vitally urgent!

A GROWING CONCERN ABOUT THE FATE OF THE JEWS

My concern for the Jewish people in the Land of the North grew even greater when my wife, Michal Ann, began to have consistent, vivid dreams about a new European holocaust. Many of her dreams have come to pass. I fell to my knees in even greater intercession for my Jewish brothers in the Land of the North and other nations. This is what Michal Ann saw in one of her dramatic dreams in the summer of 2000:

> I saw thousands of Jews trying to escape from within European countries. In this dream, they were not trying to escape only through to Finland and across the North Sea to England; they were trying to head south through Italy to the Mediterranean Sea. It included Russia, Germany, France, Austria and the whole European scene.
>
> These countries were providing transportation so the Jews could escape, but their policy toward anyone who wanted to pursue the Jews was, "Whoever wants to go after them may do so. However many you kill is fine. Our official statement is that we are allowing them to

leave and we are providing transportation. Whatever happens to them in transit is not our responsibility."

There were many different modes of escape, but in every case I saw tremendous numbers of people being killed. It was just horrible. I saw railway boxcars filled with Jewish people—just like the images we have of the Jews herded into Nazi boxcars during the Holocaust of World War II. They were packed like sardines.

In some cases, it seemed like someone had purposely pulled out old train cars from the Holocaust time frame in World War II; then they made these Jews get in the same boxcars.

They had also rigged the sliding doors to these boxcars so they could not be closed. Then I saw automobiles filled with modern neo-Nazis in uniforms driving up alongside these train cars and killing as many people as they could with their guns.

At a later point, I saw that only a handful of Jews had survived the train trip. I also noticed that in some of the boxcars hangman's nooses had been tied up to their supporting beams. There were as many as 50 nooses in a car, and some of them had been used to hang Jewish victims. Their bodies were cut down, but the Nazis left the end of the noose hanging in the boxcars to terrorize all the people who would try to escape in the future.

They also used a taxidermy procedure on three Jewish bodies, and their stuffed skins hung in the nooses. Anyone riding in the boxcars was jostled by the carcasses throughout the train ride. I remember riding in one of the cars and bumping up against one of those bodies while looking into its face. It was just horrible.

Then the scene changed and I saw Jewish people trying to escape in automobiles. Once again I saw carloads of uniformed neo-Nazis pulling alongside them. The

Jews were fleeing for their lives, and they had little to fight with.

I remember one carload of Jewish people in particular because they actually fought back with some boat oars that they had found. The only thing they could figure out to do was to wait until these Nazi soldiers had pulled up alongside.

When the neo-Nazis pulled up alongside the Jews, they rolled down the window to point their guns. The Jews stuck their boat oars through the window and jabbed them into the chests of the soldiers, crushing their sternums. In their desperation, they had no choice but to brutally defend themselves.

Every time the Jews tried to defend themselves, it was with hand tools and in hand-to-hand combat. The enemy always had cars and guns to fight with.

It seemed as though Italy had decided to open up a portion of their border to let the Jews go through. Many, though, were still being killed, thousands upon thousands. I found myself praying in the dream, "Open the door, open the door and let them go!"

Finally the few straggling refugees who made it through the gauntlet of escape seemed to arrive at their destination—a large green pasture that was totally surrounded by a dense planting of scrubby oak trees. In one way it seemed like it could be a good defensive place, but to me what seemed to be the issue was that those trees constricted a possible path of escape should one become necessary. And there was a foreboding sense that the neo-Nazis were still following, and that there was no real security at all.

I was one of these refugees along with two of my children, because in the dream, I was Jewish. We experienced these things alongside the Jewish people.

There were some empty rough cabins provided, but I do not know if there were even any small cots or blankets there. It just seemed that everything they had were the things they had brought with them.

This was definitely a dream about the Jews being hunted, but it had a twisted "sporting edge" to it. The Nazis let them think that they were escaping, but they were really just playing a mental game with them.

The enemy let them run while driving them with fear. They wanted to see how many they could track down and kill, and they wanted to see how they would react.[14]

I am convinced that God sometimes gives us glimpses of unpleasant things, not to paralyze us with fear but to energize us to pray in faith. I am convinced that we are destined to relive the book of Esther in this generation! The more I prayed and sought God's face, the more I began to sense a prophetic word rising in my heart for the nations concerning the need for an Esther anointing and a Mordecai anointing in the Church.

A Fresh Focus on Esther

In February 2000, I spoke at The Lord of the Harvest conference in Hanover, Germany. The event's theme came from the Lord's words, "Therefore beseech the Lord of the harvest to send out workers into His harvest" (Matt. 9:38).

I was slated to speak each of the first two nights of the three-night event. However, in a dream I had before I traveled to Hanover, the meeting on the second night took a different direction because of the weighty presence of the Spirit of the Lord during the worship time. I also saw that I would be given "a trumpet to blast" on the third night. This was not a desire on my part to have more time at the podium. I speak so often in so many places that my itch to preach was scratched many years ago.

Statue in Prague

As I had dreamed, on the second night of the conference, the anointing of God settled upon us as we worshiped. Many in the audience were on their faces, seeking the Lord as His presence was equally sweet and convicting. His presence was among His people.

In that atmosphere of high anointing, I felt led to read the book of Esther in its entirety. I had read it scores of times before, but never under these circumstances. Within the first few verses, I realized I was seeing Esther's story with a different set of spiritual lenses. This time I focused on Mordecai instead of Esther. The Lord wanted me to see and understand the role Mordecai played in that time of crisis. Sure enough, I was asked to address the conference on the third night. When I spoke, I told the people, "Rarely do I stand in what I would call the 'office of a prophet' to give a word to a nation. But I believe the Lord would have me give a prophetic word to the nation of Germany."

It was clear to me that God wanted to raise up Mordecais for this generation to prepare Esther, figuratively representing the corporate Church in its proper role as deliverer and intercessor for the Jewish people. If there had been no Mordecai, there would have been no Esther. If there had been no Esther, a genocide of a generation would have occurred!

The Season Is About to Change

A change of season is approaching. The time is not yet here, but it is coming. It is right at the door! The Holy Spirit wants to inject the burden of the Lord for purposes of God among the Jewish people into the global prayer movement, like a nurse with a fully loaded needle. We need a potent injection of God's heart into our heart! That is why God wants to raise up a Mordecai anointing to prepare Esther for *a time of intervention*. We know what Esther accomplished, but what was Mordecai's task? What was his divine assignment?

Mordecai's job was to raise up and prepare Esther for her hour of influence before the king. Mordecai raised Esther as his own daughter. He did not bow down or pay homage to Haman, who sought the destruction of the Jews, but only worshiped the one true God. He intercepted Haman's scheme of the enemy and revealed it with wisdom to those in authority. He walked in prophetic counsel and instilled courage into Esther.

Esther, properly tutored and mentored by the counsel of Mordecai, seized the moment through prayer and fasting. She launched an all-out appeal to the king for the deliverance of the Jews from their sworn enemy. Esther was anointed to intervene and stand in the gap, yet she had to walk in cooperation with the preparation of Mordecai, the spiritual authority God placed in her life. Her intervention would not have succeeded unless she had first cooperated.

We Must Learn to Walk Together

Prayer gave her the right of approach, helping create the favor that extended the scepter of grace, and gave her privileged access to the supreme earthly authority over Persia and the Jews, the king. God was the true authority, but He chose to work through Mordecai to alert Esther to her destiny and the timing of her intercessory acts on behalf of the Jews.

In a critical hour, intercessors and those in authority (spiritual and secular) *must learn to walk together*. Today, as in Esther's day, there are millions of lives at stake.

Just as intercessors cannot afford to walk an independent road, so must spiritual leaders avoid the temptation to walk and lead in exclusivity, reserving their outreach, leadership and spiritual resources solely for their own gatherings. A marriage must occur between the watchmen on the walls and the gatekeepers of every city.

The gatekeepers are elders who sit at the gates. They are to become gatekeepers of His presence. Watchmen on the walls are to watch and see what the Lord is doing locally and among the nations. Watchmen are posted in high places to watch every route of approach and announce ahead of time the identity and purpose of those who approach the community of God— whether the visitors are ambassadors of goodwill or enemies approaching with evil intent.

Watchmen do not always have the authority to apply the revelation or even at times to issue the warnings—their revelation and intercession must be submitted to the governmental authorities who sit at the gates by God's design. These gatekeepers, both secular and spiritual leaders, then must determine whether to bar the gates or to open them wide. *No matter what opinions or experiences we may have, it is clear from God's Word that these two essential ministries must learn to walk together.*

The Russians Are Coming

On the third night of the meeting in Hanover, after a sanctified time in God's presence at the close of my message, I gave a word to Germany: "The Russians are coming." I explained that a *God-sent* Russian invasion of Jews was about to descend on the nation. It would be their opportunity to "rewrite history." I stood in brokenness, reminding the audience that German people and the slumbering Church worldwide had slaughtered the Jews before—but we could give them safe harbor today and in the future. It was one of the few times I have given a prophetic word to an entire nation, yet God commanded me to issue a Mordecai and Esther call.

Chuck Pierce, who has served as the executive director of the World Prayer Center and vice president of Global Harvest, and I talked about this word. His response shook me to the core of my being. He was in Europe when he sent me this e-mail message:

Since I am here in Europe, I will pray through this issue. One strong word we received before leaving on this trip had to do with *Haman—how* [he] *was waiting and watching.* I have pondered it much. Therefore, I will believe with you that *the Mordecai and Esther anointing will begin to arise* all across Europe to overthrow the noose being prepared.

The other portion of the word was, "Tell Esther not to come forth until Mordecai releases her and tells her when." I will pray about timing.[15]

Esther's three-day fast was an urgent act of crisis intervention. She and Mordecai observed a total fast from food and drink of any kind. No one casually enters into this kind of a fast. A life-and-death crisis is a good reason; so is a direct command from God.

A Historic Window of Opportunity

People gifted with prophetic vision and insight understand that Jewish people, in particular Russian Jews, are approaching another season of crisis. This is *our* chance to rewrite history, too—this is not something limited to German believers. This is a historic global window of opportunity for the Church to arise and wash the stains and spots out of our bridal garment.

I have a mandate and heavenly burden to release a cry and divine declaration: Let the Mordecais and Esthers of the Church come forth. Let these men and women take their stand for God and for the Jewish people. There is no better time than *now!* We were born, anointed and set in place for "such a time as this."

The Church must throw out life preservers of prayer and fasting to save the Russian Jews who are at risk of being overtaken by a rising flood of unreasoning anti-Semitism. I am *not* talking about something that is going to come—it has already begun. In fact, it is spiraling out of control in hot spots around the world, especially in the former Soviet bloc.

When we speak comfort to God's Covenant People, we honor Him. We want the Jewish people to discover and receive their Messiah; but one of the first steps is to reach out in prayer, fasting, love, compassion and practical assistance, particularly to help them safely return to their ancient home of Israel.

Serious crises call for serious strategies. Unbridled attacks from the enemy require our most powerful weapons of warfare. Desperate times demand desperate measures!

We must somehow tap into deeper veins of prayer. Such a longing has compelled me to look back at historic times of effective crisis intercession. What was it that worked for our spiritual ancestors when they faced their most difficult trials? I found some answers in Wales.

A Visit with Samuel Howells

Trevor and Sharon Baker, friends of mine who live in England, had graduated from Swansea Bible College, also known as the Bible College of Wales. They arranged for me to meet with Samuel Howells, the only living son and successor of the great intercessor, Rees Howells.

Sue Kellough, a proven prophetess who serves on the board of directors for my ministry, Ministry to the Nations, came with me. Kellough also heads Builders, Incorporated, a prophetic intercessory ministry in Indianapolis, Indiana.

Howells, who had succeeded his father as president of the Bible college, was 86 years old when we had tea with him on the Swansea campus. He showed us "the blue room" where many historic prayer meetings had taken place during the dark years of World War II. The tea was attended by an elderly lady who had participated in all of those prayer gatherings.

Before the door had opened in Wales, I had already visited other places on the historic crisis intercession map. I had led a group to Hernhut, Germany, the site of the Moravian Community and Prayer Movement that conducted an unprecedented round-the-clock prayer watch that was unbroken for more than 100 years. The Holy Spirit had descended upon the Moravians in an unforgettable manifestation of divine impartation.[16]

It became clear that, this time (in the twenty-first century) the Lord had another plan. This was to be a quieter, personal impartation. Why He would choose such a strategy soon became apparent.

A Proven Anointing

During our "divine appointment" in Wales, I asked Howells some vital questions, knowing that his family and the intercessors at the college had a proven anointing to pray for intervention.

In his book *Rees Howells: Intercessor*, author Norm Grubb recounts how Howells and students at Swansea Bible College had interceded during crucial moments at the end of World War II. They received divine revelation about Nazi movements and aerial invasion schemes, then prayed, using the writings of the Old Testament prophets. At the last minute, Nazi bombers turned back without any apparent reason. "There seemed no reason why the Luftwaffe should have turned home, just at the moment when victory was in their grasp," records the Swansea Bible College website. "But we know why."[17]

The Key to Authority in Prayer

As soon as we settled down to tea, I asked, "Mr. Samuel [the proper way to address Samuel Howells in Wales], how is it that your father got this revelation? How did he and the people know what to pray for? I know it was not by newspaper [reports] and I know it was not by radio. How did he know what armies were in what locations? How did he know what battles to pray through and when? Did it come by dreams or visions? How did it come?"

The son of the great intercessor turned to me and simply said, "Don't you think it is time for another crumpet?"

Howells did not immediately answer my question. He freely talked about other things. He answered questions and carried on a dialogue without hesitation, but his demeanor changed when I turned to him again and asked, "Mr. Samuel, how is it that your father and all the intercessors in that period of time knew what to pray for? What was the key of authority that the Lord gave you for intervention in that period of time?"

Again, Howells looked at me and said, "Don't you think it is time for a little more tea?"

It was if he did not hear the question I asked and would not give the answers I yearned to hear.

I grew bolder. A third time I inquired, "Mr. Samuel, *I must know!* Did an angel come and announce these things? How did they know? Did it happen by spiritual gifts or through illumination of the written Word? How did they know of the battles and when and how to pray?"

Still there was no answer. "Enough of this," Howells said, refusing to satisfy my query.

Possessed by God

Then Sue Kellough, older and more tenacious than I, approached Howells. She dropped to her knees, peered up at the veteran intercessor and gave it one last try: "Mr. Samuel, our nation is in great need, and [with] the days that lie in front of us, we are in great need of the kind of prayer that your father and you and these people have known in the past."

A tear trickled down his cheek as he looked into our eyes: "You must understand, the Lord's servant [that is how he referred to his father] was possessed by God."

Kellough and I wept. Then we asked Howells to pray for us. Later we learned that Howells rarely meets with people, and I have been told that he does not pray for people when he does meet with them. Nevertheless, he laid his hands upon us and asked the Lord to grant to us the authority of "identification" and "intercession."

He asked the Lord to give us the place of purity in prayer, that our hearts would become aligned with God's purposes and that we would pray out of God's heart. He prayed very simply, concluding with the prayer that it would all be centered in Jesus.

Greater Than a Prayer Technique

I left Swansea Bible College knowing I had taken part in a divine appointment. This was greater than a mere prayer technique. It is even higher than a paper or book promising "eleven effective steps to answered prayer." Howells reluctantly shared with me a truth that very few people are willing to implement in their lives: The most effectual fervent prayer comes when the Lord Himself takes *possession* of His people. We are not our own. We were bought at a price. We are being called to be *possessed with and by God*. This revelation answered all of my questions about the secret of effective crisis intercession.

I later came across the text of a letter from Dr. Kingsley Priddy of Swansea Bible College. It was reproduced in the appendix of Gustav Scheller's book *Operation Exodus*:

> You see Intercession is not prayer, nor even very intense prayer. Anyone may pray, and pray earnestly, for something, and yet not be committed to be irrevocably responsible, at any cost, for it's fulfillment. The intercessor is.
>
> In Intercession there is Identification with the matter or persons interceded for. The intercessor is willing to take the place of the one prayed for; to let *their* need become *his* need; to let *their* need be met at *his* expense and to let *their* suffering become the travail of *his* own heart.
>
> That is how the Lord Jesus "*made intercession for the transgressors*" (Isaiah 53:12). "*He was numbered with the*

transgressors," and "*He was wounded for* (their) *transgressions*" (v. 5). He had to be "identified" with sinners; He secured their pardon by vicariously paying the debt that they owed.[18]

TIME TO CARRY THE BATON

All of what has happened in recent years brings me to the burning question of this book: Has God ordained that a trumpet be sounded?

Mordecai and Esther are gone. The season of Joseph Rabinowitz is over. Will someone in this generation step forward to shout and signal to his shipwrecked people to flee to the Rock? As each generation passes on, another must carry the baton. The Holy One of Israel is once again looking for a man, for a woman, for people to stand in the gap on behalf of His ancient Covenant People, the Jews.

A Call for a Yearly Esther Fast

It is time that we cry out to the Church around the world with a solemn call to a yearly fast, an Esther Fast for the salvation and preservation of the Jewish people in the Land of the North and around the world. In the name of Jesus Christ, I call forth the Mordecais to prepare Esther, which is the Church, for her greatest hour of selfless intercession for the Jewish people.

The antichrist spirit of Haman has loosed a fresh plot to destroy the Jews of today. God is seeking Mordecais and Esthers to step forward. He is calling people of prayer to stand in the gap in this generation. True deliverance comes in the realm of the Spirit, not in the realm of man. God is offering an opportunity for the Body of Christ to arise. A window of opportunity has opened enabling the Church to rewrite history before the throne of almighty God. I was born for this. I was born again for this. So were you!

Signs and Wonders Will Follow

When God delivered Israel from Egypt with the first Great Exodus, He did it through sovereign acts of supernatural intervention. The Hebrews were not delivered from pharaoh's grip by swords, chariots or mighty armies—they were delivered by God's hand. *Supernatural signs and wonders were the tools of their release!*

Most of the Jews who have made aliyah since World War II did not arrive in Israel through signs and wonders. Jews have migrated to Israel by plane and by ship. They have made their exodus because of the sacrifices of men. A few miracles occurred along the way, but most of the breakthroughs happened as a result of hard work and astute maneuvering through political mazes.

God will continue to use all of these means. There have been in the past and will continue to be in our generation multiple phases of His great work. But my strong conviction is that the completion of the Second Great Exodus is destined to eclipse the first, and it will again come about through the supernatural contending of altars.

We see "the altar of the occult and the demonic" rising around the world. At the same time, the authentic staff of God is being lifted through the prayers and selfless obedience of the Church. The supernatural authority of God will once again swallow up the counterfeit powers of the enemy.

The Closing of an Era

Perhaps the present era of the fishers is coming to a close. Maybe another era of the hunters is already beginning. As it was in Egypt during the first Great Exodus, the Jewish people will be pushed out by the hands of the hunters and by the prophetic and the apostolic display of great signs and wonders—all for the glory of God. Yes, all for the glory of His holy name.

We have already seen miracle after miracle come to pass on behalf of the Russian Jews in response to prayer in recent years.

There is no other explanation for the rapid disintegration of the world's second-ranked superpower. There is no other rationale for the fall of the Berlin Wall after decades of unrestrained terror and bondage.

"Let My People Go!"

With great power and authority, God's people are declaring to the Land of the North: "Let My people go, let My people go!" At such a time as this, we must ask: Where are the Corrie ten Booms and Fritz Graebes, the righteous Gentiles of our day who are willing to so closely identify with the plight of the Jewish people that they will put themselves on the line to see them saved and preserved from destruction? Where are the Dietrich Bonhoeffers who will stand up and declare the truth about God's love for the Jews, even in the face of public disapproval and personal danger? This is the very heart of God for this generation!

Are we willing to stand and make a difference? Now is the time for Mordecai to rise up and for Esther to be prepared. We need to call forth the same anointing for crisis intercession that was upon Rees Howells at Swansea Bible College during World War II. *Without it we perish!*

I have a word: We must get possessed by God! Do we want to be close to the heart of God? Then we need to love the things that He loves, specifically His Covenant People. We have to catch the Mordecai anointing and be people who prepare the corporate Esther, the Church, for this critical time. We can rewrite history before the throne of God!

CHAPTER 9

THE CRY—
IT IS TIME TO TAKE
ACTION!

With weeping they will come, and by supplication I will lead them.

JEREMIAH 31:9

After the fall of Communism, I made several trips into Czechoslovakia. On my second visit, in 1991, after ministering at a national conference in Prague, my friends and I went to Libreac, a city in the northern part of the nation. In Libreac we met a Moravian pastor named Evald Ruffy. He was unable to attend the national gathering because he had just been released from the hospital.

Ruffy had suffered a heart attack and fallen into a coma.[1] People across Czechoslovakia and also in Sweden, where he was hospitalized, prayed and cried out to the Lord. Ruffy's wife and his associate pastor rushed to the hospital, where they, too, interceded.

A VISION IN HEAVEN

For three days, the doctors and the intercessors struggled to save Ruffy's life. During this time, Ruffy says, he was in heaven where he was told about future events that would take place on Earth. He saw a picture of Central and Eastern Europe covered with dark clouds. White lights went up and down, breaking apart the dark clouds.

"What is this?" Ruffy inquired.

"The dark clouds are 'territorial spirits' ruling over those regions and the white lights are the Lord's angels at work to break them up and push them back," his guide, the Holy Spirit, replied.

Ruffy asked another question, "How does this happen?" The answer came quickly: "This happens in response to the prayers of the saints."

During Ruffy's visit to heaven, he was also shown a white bridge. It stretched from Ethiopia to Israel, arching through the clouds. Ruffy saw 15,000 black men and women walk across the bridge into the Promised Land. He inquired, "What is this?" God answered: "These are My ancient Jewish people whom I will bring home from Ethiopia to Israel."

Ruffy prodded even further: "How does this come to pass?" The Holy Spirit explained, "Why, this, too, happens in answer to the prayers of the saints."

As Ruffy's body lay in his hospital bed and his spirit walked through heaven, he became aware that he was a husband, a father and a pastor. He sensed that his work on Earth was not yet complete. As the associate pastor interceded, tears hit Ruffy's face. At that moment, he knew he had to make a choice!

Moments later, Ruffy saw his spirit soar through the heavens and rejoin his body. He was instantly healed! The doctors declared it a miracle and released him from the hospital. He did not even have to pay the medical bill.

Just a few weeks after Ruffy's visit to heaven and his miraculous healing, what the Holy Spirit had revealed became a reality. In what was called Operation Solomon, round-the-clock rescue missions airlifted about 15,000 black Ethiopian Jews from Addis Ababa, Ethiopia, to Tel Aviv, Israel. I remember praying through the prophetic passage of Ezekiel 34:29-30 at the time. That Scripture passage declares:

"I will establish for them a renowned planting place, and
they will not again be victims of famine in the land, and
they will not endure the insults of the nations any more.
Then they will know that I, the LORD their God, am with
them, and that they, the house of Israel, are My people,"
declares the LORD God.

THE THREE MINISTRIES BROUGHT TOGETHER

The Lord has given me a burden to see the Body of Christ
function in unity. I yearn to see three strands (the prophetic
movement, the global prayer movement and missions endeavors) work together. When interlaced, the three strands would
form a single, strong cord that could not be torn apart. What
a powerful weapon that would be when put in the Lord's
hands!

The Prophetic Movement

Prophecy is a threefold gift. It is partial, progressive and condi-
tional. First of all, even the best prophesy only "in part" (1 Cor.
13:9). But when we bring the various pieces together, like a giant
jigsaw puzzle, we can unearth the whole picture! However, fit-
ting the pieces together only occurs when we seek confirmation
and godly counsel.

Most authentic words do not appear overnight. They are
progressive. They arrive one step at a time. The first few install-
ments might not look like the entire revelation, but when we
wait upon the Lord, we often see that indeed caterpillars turn
into butterflies!

Often, before the beauty of the entire promise of God
unfolds, certain conditions must be met. Sometimes God does
not reveal these conditions, but they must still be fulfilled. Many

times, we must seek the Lord to discover what conditions He requires before He unlocks the prophetic potential!

The Global Prayer Movement

The global prayer movement is growing up. Watches of the Lord and Houses of Prayer have been established around the world. Prayer walkers march forward and intercessors coordinate 10/40 and 40/70 prayer windows that target specific regions of the world. The call to 40 days of fasting has been embraced by hundreds of thousands of people from various streams in the Body of Christ.

The Lord has used forerunners to establish His works in the twenty-first century Church. Men of God such as Hudson Taylor, Rees Howells and Gustav Scheller have laid the groundwork. Now it is our turn to pick up the baton of effective prayer. We need local churches to climb aboard the prayer movement. We must see local prayer teams combine the prophetic and intercessory. We must help all believers grow until they are functioning as intercessory priests. We cannot settle for anything less!

God wants us to remind Him of His Word. When we go before His throne, we should Kneel on the Promises He has made and pray them back to Him. We must embrace and apply the truths of identificational repentance. As we hold off judgment, we clear the way for His will to come tumbling down to planet Earth. We must learn to cry out together: "Father, forgive us!" Then our land will be healed!

Missions Endeavors

As we enter the twenty-first century, God is birthing a new apostolic movement. We will see the greatest church-planting effort in history. Unlike the previous raping of the nations that often happened in the name of Christ, this missions outreach will bless the nations as authentic, indigenous works emerge.

Fervent troops of young people are about to be released on the missions scene. God will use them to accomplish powerful exploits. They will be "fire carriers" who love the poor, love the cross of Jesus and declare His praises in the streets. The hearts of fathers will turn back to their children and the hearts of the children will turn back toward the older generations (Mal. 4:6).

Awakened or Messianic Sephardic Jews who now live in diaspora throughout much of Latin America will be at the center of this church-planting movement. In chapter 3, we read about the Spanish Inquisition and the fate of Jews in Europe. It is now time to rewrite those wrongs of the past.

As God moves upon these Sephardic Jews, they will retrace the trail their ancestors took from Europe to the new world. They will converge upon Spain and Portugal, where such evil atrocities prevailed in past centuries. Once back in their native lands, these Messianic Sephardic Jews will take part in radical acts of intercession. They will break generational curses, extend prayers of forgiveness for past wrongs and reclaim what Satan has stolen. *Empowered by the Holy Spirit, they will write a new page of history.*

Some missiologists have suggested that the final frontier of evangelism targets Islam and Hinduism. Certainly these veils of darkness will be pierced. But I contend that the final frontier will be taken by empowered Hebrew Christians. When these Messianic apostolic evangelists march forth as broken vessels, the devil will tremble.

LET'S REWRITE HISTORY!

Large portions of the global Church failed through their manifest weakness and inaction during World War II. We must not fall into the trap of fear and apathy again. We can yet rewrite Church history! We were brought to the Kingdom for such a time as this, a time to issue a great Exodus Cry in the power of the Holy Spirit and in the name of Jesus Christ.

This will require a *supernatural* Church, not merely a religious institution that can be produced and maintained through programs and procedures apart from the presence and transforming power of God. This end-times intercessory mission calls for an unparalleled apostolic and prophetic movement of a radical last-days Church! Though a complicated statement, this truly defines what the Church of the living God must become.

The Church was and is apostolic, in the sense that it is established upon the "foundation of the apostles and prophets."[2] It is *sent* to take territory. We do this when we plant churches and establish new works to expand the kingdom of God in the earth. The Church is also sent to bring divine order to godless chaos through the authority and name of the Prince of Peace, Jesus.

We need a revolutionary apostolic movement because God is doing something that defies and transcends every national, ethnic and political border known among men. It will even go beyond the denominational walls that we have worked so long to construct and maintain.

This apostolic reformation must spring from a *radical* Church in this end-times season. It must be a Church with all of the characteristics, power and anointing demonstrated in the first-century Church of the book of Acts.

This type of Church is not a powerless monolith preserving the lifeless vestiges of a dead religion, like some museum of failed faith. Rather, this is the Church of the living God that moves in supernatural signs and wonders! When God's Word is declared, the Lord Himself will confirm it through signs and wonders.[3]

Finally, the Church must *lead the way* in this crisis confronting the Russian Jews and the Jewish people in other parts of the world.

In previous centuries, the Church sat back in fear or apathy—even worse, it took the lead in persecuting the Jewish people in ignorance or outright hatred. Never again. This time, we will take the lead in crisis intercession and intervention, carrying the Jews on our shoulders in fulfillment of the ancient prophecy: "Thus says the Lord GOD, 'Behold, I will lift up My hand to the nations and set up My standard to the peoples; and they will bring your sons in *their* bosom, and your daughters will be carried on *their* shoulders'" (Is. 49:22, emphasis mine).

IT'S TIME TO TAKE ACTION!

The crisis is clear, but *is prayer enough?* Is that *all* God calls us to do? The question should be, "Is there enough prayer?" S. D. Gordon said: "You can do more than pray after you've prayed, but you cannot do more than pray *until* you've prayed."[4]

Daniel added urgency to the one-two punch of prayer and deeds when he wrote, "The people who know their God will *display strength* and *take action*" (Dan. 11:32, emphasis mine).

We must have five vital components to fulfill this particular mandate of God on the modern Church.

1. Discernment. In this age of transition, we must be shrewd as serpents and innocent as doves. Natural perception is powerless against demonic deception. If we seek Him and ask for wisdom, He will give us the ability to discern the times like the sons of Issachar, who were praised for their ability to understand the times and discern the will of God.[5]

We need to add the jewels of wisdom and discernment to our bridal tiara. Let's seek the Lord so we can rediscover these missing gems. Ask the Lord to remove blinders of religious pride and arrogance from our eyes. We must obtain and apply eye salve at this hour so that our sight can be healed! Inquire of the Lord so that the eyes of our hearts will be enlightened with the spirit of wisdom and revelation (see Eph. 1:17-19).

2. Preparation. The Scriptures are filled with counsel to the wise, urging us to prepare for things we perceive are coming our way. That means we prepare for the changing seasons (we prepare for winter by storing away food and supplies), we prepare for traps (by taking steps to avoid them) and we prepare for war (by training and counting the potential cost). This biblical mandate particularly applies to our preparations for the final return of the King of kings and Lord of lords to the earth. When we receive a warning or assignment from God, it is *our* responsibility to prepare for it in advance using every means we have at our disposal.

For decades, faithful believers have gathered and secretly stored supplies vital to the survival and comfort of refugees— particularly for Russian Jewish people fleeing the Land of the North. There are storehouses and secret shelters hidden in Finland, Norway, Sweden, Denmark, England, Iceland and throughout Europe awaiting the flood of Jews making aliyah. This time, the Church will *not* fail to bless and protect the Jewish people in Christ's name. Will you arise with me and take action?

3. Financial Commitment. By faith, leaders such as Gustav Scheller, Jonathan Bernis, John Hagee, Derek Prince, Sid Roth and many others have motivated the Church in countless nations to *invest* their money as well as their prayers in the deliverance and final exodus of the Russian Jews.

An immense exodus has already taken place, but the exodus ahead of us will eclipse everything the world has ever seen! The Scriptures tell us, and the prophets confirm, that as the hunters are released in the former Soviet states and Europe, the Jewish people who remain will suddenly run for safety. When that Second Great Exodus takes place, God wants us to be ready to greet them with food, clothing, shelter, transportation and whatever assistance they need. All of these things cost money.

Statue in Saint Petersburg, Russia

One Christmas, our family of two adults and four children took up an offering as part of our worship to the Lord. We celebrated the birth of Jesus by giving financially to a ministry to help fly a Russian-Jewish couple to their new homeland in Israel. We did this gladly, because we knew it was what the Lord would want us to do.

When you stand before the judgment seat of Christ, and the Lord asks you, "What did you do for these my brothers?" What will you say?

There are many organizations and efforts you can support, including the ones mentioned in appendix 5. It is vital to give now while the window of opportunity is still ajar!

4. The Word of God. One of the most spiritual ways to help these Jewish pilgrims is to provide the life-giving truth of the New Testament to them in Russian, a language most of them speak. Rabbi Richard Glickstein, who now resides in Finland with his family, at one time lived in Moscow. He currently directs a project to raise finances for the publishing of a Russian-language New Testament that is styled for Jewish readers.

This Harvest Bible Project uses a translation by David H. Stern called *The Jewish New Testament*. I own a copy and read it. This translation of Scripture is excellent and insightful!

While calling forth prayer is essential, we must also do exploits in Yeshua's name! Just as doctors need medicine and builders need lumber, Christian relief workers need appropriate "bridge tools" to help introduce these Jewish people to their Messiah! Give life by giving these precious people the Word of life in their own language. Invest, along with me and others, in this wonderful Harvest Bible Project.

5. Radical Prayer and Fasting. Times of crisis call for crisis intercession. By any definition, this kind of prayer is an extreme action! Radical prayer is insistent, Bible-based and inspired by faith. Our Lord Jesus described it as the "persistent widow" refusing to give the judge rest until he hears and answers her cry.[6]

In this story, a widow cries for justice and legal protection from her opponent. As never before, the Jewish people need justice and legal protection from their dark opponent and ancient adversary, Satan. As Daniel once did, we are to cry out and fast before God on behalf of the Jewish people (see Dan. 9:3). We must be persistent so that once again, the archangel Michael will be released to protect and preserve the descendants of Abraham, Isaac and Jacob.

The lost weapon of fasting is being recovered by the Church. Truly effective crisis intercession is launched from the biblical foundation of fasting. God's Word provides the greatest examples in Esther and Mordecai, who called a solemn three-day fast from all food and drink in a time of life-and-death crisis (see the book of Esther in the Old Testament). Once again, God is calling us to an Esther Fast on behalf of His ancient Covenant People. First we deal with the principality and power behind the hunters, then we offer practical, loving support to help the Russian Jews rediscover their identity, find places of refuge throughout the world, return to their homeland and meet their promised Messiah.

LAUNCHING "THE CRY"

When should we observe an Esther Fast? The fast called by Clyde Williamson (see chapter 5) coincided with Purim, the Jewish holy day observing God's great redemption of the Jewish people from Haman's plot to destroy them. Jewish people traditionally incorporate an Esther Fast with their celebration of Purim in honor of Queen Esther, who led a fast in her day. Therefore, Purim is a great time to intercede against the plots and schemes of the modern-day spirit of Haman. It is the perfect occasion to request safety and salvation of the Jewish people.

According to the Jewish calendar, Purim is held in the month of *Adar*, which usually falls in February or March. Moses was born in Adar. It is also the month when the Jewish leader Maccabees defeated the Syrians and the month when the orders were given to rebuild the walls of Jerusalem preceding the reconstruction of the Temple and first return of the Jewish people to Israel. (Dates for the feast of Purim, according to the Julian calendar, appear in appendix 3. Supporting Scriptures are listed in appendix 4.)

In earlier chapters of this book, we looked at the historical accounts of the persecution of the Jewish people from the time of the Inquisition in Spain to Hitler's brutal murder of about 6 million unarmed Jewish men, women and children. We chronicled current-day attacks on the Jewish people in Europe and the United States. *Can you hear "the word of the Lord" on this crisis?* Now is the time to pray, fast and do great exploits through the power of God. Nothing less will do. Anything short of the mark will only produce the same type of harvest we saw in World War II. We must say, "Never again!"

Unlocking Historic Action

The prophetic promise is our invitation from God into priestly intercession. When we seek the heart of God concerning the Jewish people and their destiny, we unlock historic action.

Join me, and millions of other Christians, by stepping into the prophetic purposes of God for this generation! Lift your voice in prophetic crisis intercession for the Jewish people around the world. Let the Church arise and intercede in Jesus' name. Let's step forward in unity for the deliverance of Jewish people who live in the Land of the North.

Precious brothers and sisters blazed a trail of faithfulness before us in this intercessory burden. We have taken a glance at a few of them, including the selfless work of Clyde Williamson, who trumpeted the Esther Fast Mandate and marshaled the intercessors and financial resources of the Church more than a decade ago when the Communists still held the Russian Jews in a death grip. But God is raising new voices and new runners are coming into the race to grasp the baton and carry it through the next leg in this strategic marathon race.

With the burden of the Lord as one of the modern-day Mordecais, I now feel the necessity to reemphasize and reinstate this solemn season of fasting and prayer. We must take radical action until we see God's ancient Covenant People delivered from the Land of the North and transported safely to their biblical homeland, Eretz Israel. We must press even further until the eyes of these Jewish people have been opened to behold their Messiah, Yeshua.

Therefore, every year, I am calling on Christians to sacrifice our time, our comfort and our agendas to undertake a three-day Esther Fast at Purim. This spiritual investment of the Worldwide Prayer Movement in the global Body of Christ will not fail. It will bring about nothing less than "God's will on earth as it is in heaven" for the Jewish people and the nation of Israel.

Once again, recall the prophetic declaration of Jeremiah the prophet:

> "Therefore behold, days are coming," declares the LORD, "when it will no longer be said, 'As the LORD lives, who brought up the sons of Israel out of the land of Egypt,' but, 'As the LORD lives, who brought up the sons of Israel from the land of the north and from all the countries where He had banished them.' For I will restore them to their own land which I gave to their fathers. Behold, I am going to send for many fishermen," declares the LORD, "and they will fish for them; and afterwards I will send for many hunters, and they will hunt them from every mountain and every hill and from the clefts of the rocks" (Jer. 16:14-16).

This prophetic passage clearly warns that after the fishers come many hunters. Perhaps the time of the fishers is nearing an end and the time of the hunters has already begun. It is time for the Church to tap its supernatural source, leading the Jewish people to safety through trials, tears, supplication, prophetic appeal and an amazing time of signs and wonders. Write it down and watch it come to pass: The completion of the Second Great Exodus shall occur in a time of intense pressure, trials, supplications and an unparalleled move of God with signs and wonders!

ARE THE HUNTERS REALLY COMING?

What about the word I received that gave a time line of 18 months before another group of hunters would be released? Two things have happened:

- By an extreme act of God's love and mercy, the Goll family has moved to a place of seclusion just as God told me we would. It was a symbolic and prophetic act declaring His call to His people to find Him as their hiding place.
- At the end of those 18 months, in the fall of 2000, a new, heightened level of violence erupted inside Israel's borders. Also at this time, the number of Russian Jews making aliyah came to a virtual standstill, after an extended period of increased immigration. But there are many who still wish to depart, and when persecution by hunters increases, many more will need to depart.

We need to understand that the world today is potentially *more dangerous* for the Jewish people than it was when Hitler raised his army in Germany. How can that be? Some of the nations that once were part of the Communist empire known as the USSR are now in the hands of *radical Muslim leaders!* They have the potential to become virtual powder kegs of violence against the Jewish people.

Indeed, the hunters are coming. Therefore, a great mobilization is needed immediately to help Russian Jews escape from Eastern Europe and other places where persecution, threats and oppression could soon escalate.

We, the followers of Jesus Christ, must be there for the Jewish people this time. The Lord is truly opening a window of opportunity for us to right the wrongs of Church history. We can enter into this conflict through strategic intercessory prayer, by making natural provision for their protection and through financial giving. We must not miss this window of opportunity.

Let us seize the moment and arise to our destiny in an hour when persecution, tension and unrest are rampantly increasing. Let a prayer army arise and call forth the Jewish people from the Land of the North into their appointed destiny!

Practical Prayer and Action Points

- Cry out to the Lord with brokenness. Ask our Father to forgive us, the Church, for our apathy and fear which has caused us to remain silent and passive in the past.
- Ask the Lord to awaken the global Church of Jesus Christ to the immediate urgency of this message. Intercede that the Lord would raise up modern-day Mordecais, Esthers, Josephs, Daniels and Deborahs "for such a time as this."
- Pray for an extension of a time of mercy and freedom so that the Russian Jews may safely flee. Ask for the time of the fishers to continue.
- Seek protection for the Russian Jews as we transition from the time of the fishers into the time of the hunters. Pray for and prepare places of safety and refuge for Jewish people during times of persecution.

    Intercede that the enemy's plans would be thwarted and that God's destiny for the Jewish people would be fulfilled in this generation.

• Petition the Lord to increase His presence among the Jewish people with a movement of signs and wonders. Pray that the blinders would fall off of their eyes and that they would recognize and receive Jesus Christ as their sovereign Lord.

Now is the time for us to lead the way. This is the day to carry home the Jewish people on our shoulders of prayer and for us to meet their physical needs. In this way, a new generation of righteous Gentiles will demonstrate the identity of the Jewish Messiah we serve.

Now is the time for us to *pray through* the ancient prophecy of Zechariah:

I will pour out on the house of David and on the inhabitants of Jerusalem, the Spirit of grace and of supplication, so that they will look on Me whom they have pierced; and they will mourn for Him, as one mourns for an only son, and they will weep bitterly over Him like the bitter weeping over a firstborn. In that day there will be great mourning in Jerusalem, like the mourning of Hadadrimmon in the plain of Megiddo . . . In that day a fountain will be opened for the house of David and for the inhabitants of Jerusalem, for sin and for impurity (Zech. 12:10–13:1).

LET "THE CRY" ARISE

In the name of the Lord, I boldly and humbly call for the Exodus Cry, a yearly, three-day time of prayer and fasting corresponding with Purim.

Desperate times require desperate measures. It is time for the desperate prayer of the heart to arise once again! It is time to blow a trumpet in Zion. The moment has come for the Church to wash its garments in the blood of Jesus. The day has arrived for righteous sacrificial acts. Therefore, join me and many others as watchmen on the walls. Invite others to join us as well.

May this time of crisis intervention prayer and fasting for the purposes of God among the Jewish people and the nation of Israel arise until "Jerusalem is established as a praise in the earth" (Is. 62:6,7).

Remember what Jeremiah said, "With weeping they shall come, and by supplication I will lead them" (Jer. 31:9). I have a challenge for all who read this book: Whose supplications will be heard? Who will lift up their voices to fill up a golden bowl in heaven (see Rev. 5:8)? Will you join me? Let the Exodus Cry arise!

APPENDIX 1

OVERVIEW OF ISRAEL'S HISTORY

November 29, 1947. UN approves partitioning Palestine into two independent states—one Jewish and the other Arab. Arab nations renounce Jewish state and vow to seize *all* of Palestine by force.

May 14, 1948. British mandate expires. Declaration of Independence signed, proclaiming the State of Israel.

May 15, 1948. Arab nations surrounding Israel suddenly attack the world's newest nation. (This Pan-Arab force included armed forces from Egypt, Transjordan [present-day Jordan], Syria, Lebanon and Iraq.)

January 7, 1949. A cease-fire agreement ends Israel's War of Independence. (However, in an armistice agreement signed July 1949, the Arab League closes its frontiers to Israel and declares itself "in a permanent state of war" with Israel.)

January 25, 1949. The first Knesset (Parliament) meets in Jerusalem and elects Chaim Weizmann (the Jewish chemist who helped Great Britain prior to the Balfour Declaration) as its first president.

May 11, 1949. Israel is admitted to the UN.

1948-1951. Knesset enacts the Law of Return which states, "Every Jew has the right to come to this country as an immigrant." Israel's population more than doubles with 684,000 new arrivals from North Africa and the Middle East and the airlift of entire Jewish communities from Yemen (43,000) and Iraq (113,000).

1951. World Zionist Congress meets for the first time in Jerusalem.

1952-1956. West Germany signs a reparations agreement to pay the State of Israel $719 million for material losses to Jews under Nazism and $100 million to individuals. Arabs continue to be actively hostile.

3,000 clashes between armed Arab forces and Israeli soldiers.

Egypt, Syria and Jordan sign a military pact.

October 1956. Faced with Arab threats of war, Israel launches a pre-emptive attack called The Sinai Campaign, with support from Britain and France (who fear their shipping will be endangered).

March 1957. Israel withdraws from Sinai.

1958-1959. End of first decade as a new state: Jewish population reaches 1.8 million, raises the standard of living and achieves agricultural self-sufficiency. Arab and Druse communities share in progress, participate in free elections and have their own representation in the Knesset.

Israel provides technical and scientific assistance to emerging nations in Africa and Latin America—many of them establish embassies in Jerusalem and support Israel in the UN.

1967. Prelude to The Six-Day War. Al Fatah, a Palestinian terrorist organization, sends trained terrorists into Israel for sabotage. Kibbutz settlements in Galilee are bombed by Syrians.

May 14, 1967. Egyptian leader Nasser moves large numbers of troops into Sinai.

May 16-June 4, 1967. Nasser expels UN peacekeeping forces from Sinai, blocks shipping lanes in the Gulf of Aqaba and announces that Egypt is "prepared to wage war on Israel." Jordan and Iraq place their military forces under Nasser's command.

June 4, 1967. Six-Day War starts. Israel mobilizes for defense, leaving older men, women and children to keep services going, bring in agricultural harvests and pack export orders.

June 5, 1967. Israel bombs airfields of Egypt, Syria, Jordan and Iraq, destroying 452 planes in three hours! Israeli ground forces move against Egyptian forces in the Sinai at four points. Israel notifies King Hussein that it will not attack Jordan if his troops will keep the peace. In response, Jordanian troops open fire along entire armistice line and occupy UN headquarters in Jerusalem.

June 6-7, 1967. Israel counterattacks and takes all of Jerusalem, including the Old City, for the first time since A.D. 70.

June 9, 1967. Israel drives Syrians from the heavily fortified Golan Heights, penetrates Sinai to Suez Canal and takes Gaza Strip. Israeli naval forces capture Sharm el Sheikh on the Red Sea.

June 10, 1967. Cease-fire called after Israel's miraculous victory against overwhelming odds. Israel establishes following policy for occupied Arab territories: 1. guarantees free access to holy places of all three faiths; 2. takes down barriers between East and West Jerusalem; 3. begins unprecedented awakening of Jews abroad to Israel's importance for world Jewry.

1967. The War of Attrition brings on: 1. continual harassment by Egypt on Sinai borders; 2. increasing Soviet involvement in Egypt, including Soviet planes, anti-aircraft missile bases and troops.

Prelude to Yom Kippur War: 1. Egyptian and Syrian troops gather on cease-fire lines. 2. Israel begins mobilization of reserves on eve of Yom Kippur (Day of Atonement).

October 6, 1967. Yom Kippur War: 1. Israeli cabinet meets on the holy day itself, confirms Prime Minister Golda Meir's decision not to make a preemptive air strike, despite "unmistakable signs of imminent attack." The purpose is to make the responsibility for aggression unmistakably clear. 2. Arabs attack on two fronts at 2 P.M. as the Israeli cabinet is meeting.

October 7-25, 1967. Israel stops advance on both fronts within two days, but at a heavy cost.

October-November 1967. The Oil War begins after the cease-fire.

January 18, 1974. Egypt and Israel sign a disengagement agreement. U.S. officials (evidently unaware of biblical prophecy and the spiritual history of the region) claim it is the first step toward permanent Mid-East peace.

May 1974. Syria and Israel sign a disengagement agreement and Israeli forces withdraw slightly west of the cease-fire lines on the Golan Heights.

September 1975. Israel withdraws from portions of the Sinai, and Egypt reopens the Suez Canal to Israeli shipping for the first time since 1951.

January 1976. Syria takes advantage of the Lebanese civil war to move troops into Lebanon and join forces with the PLO. With much of southern Lebanon under their control, they bombard northern Israel with Soviet Ketyusha rockets.

July 1976. Israeli forces stage a daring rescue operation and free more than 100 hostages from Arab terrorists in a hijacked plane in Entebbe Airport in Uganda.

July 1977. Prime Minister Menachem Begin presents a plan for Middle East peace to U.S. President Jimmy Carter in Washington.

November 1977. Egyptian President Anwar Sadat visits Jerusalem at the invitation of Prime Minister Begin to begin direct peace talks.

September 1978. Prime Minister Begin, President Sadat and President Carter meet at Camp David, Maryland, to formulate peace accords.

March 26, 1979. Israel and Egypt sign a peace treaty. They agree to recognize and respect each other's right to live in peace within secure and recognized borders and to establish regular diplomatic relations. In response to increasing civilian casualties, Israel begins preemptive strikes against terrorist bases in southern Lebanon.

1981. PLO and Syrian forces bombard northern Israel daily, forcing residents, including children, to spend weeks in bomb shelters. Israel responds by bombing the PLO headquarters in Beirut.

January 7, 1982. Foreign Minister Yitzhak Shamir meets with Pope John Paul II.

April 25, 1982. Prime Minister Begin returns to the Sinai Peninsula to meet President Mubarak of Egypt.

June 4, 1982. The attempted assassination of Shlomo Argov, Israel's ambassador to Britain, triggers Operation Peace for Galilee, an Israeli invasion of southern Lebanon to remove the PLO's Ketyusha rockets and terrorist camps.

September 16, 1982. Lebanese Maronite-Christian soldiers enter Palestinian refugee camps in West Beirut and slaughter hundreds. One week later, 400,000 Israelis (10 percent of the entire population) gather in

~~Tel Aviv to demonstrate their horror and demand a commission of inquiry.~~

November 23, 1983. Israel trades 4,765 terrorists for 6 Israeli soldiers held prisoner by Arafat's Fatah forces.

June 28, 1984. Israel trades 291 Syrian prisoners for 11 Israeli soldiers (5 of them deceased).

January 4, 1985. Operation Moses airlifts 6,000 Ethiopian followers of Judaism to Israel.

May 20, 1985. Israel trades 1,150 terrorists for three Israeli soldiers held by Ahmed Jibril's PLO-related forces.

October 1, 1985. Israel bombs the PLO Headquarters in Tunis in response to the murder of Israeli yachters in Cyprus.

December 27, 1985. Seventeen El Al airline passengers are murdered and 109 wounded by PLO attacks at airports in Rome and Vienna.

February 11, 1986. Anatoly Sharansky, a Russian Jew active in monitoring Russian compliance with the Helsinki human rights accords, who had been imprisoned for many years in Russia's notorious labor camps, is finally freed by the USSR and arrives in Israel.

April 17, 1986. Agents of the Syrian Air Force attempt to smuggle a suitcase bomb onto an El Al London-to-Tel Aviv flight, but security guards discover and successfully dismantle the bomb.

July 22, 1986. Prime Minister Shimon Peres pays a surprise public visit to King Hassan of Morocco.

October 26, 1986. Mordechai Vanunu is hijacked back to Israel by agents of Israel's legendary Mossad security apparatus, after accepting a bribe to publicize information about Israel's purported nuclear capabilities.

February 15, 1987. Yosef Begun, a prisoner of Zion, is freed from Russian imprisonment after being sentenced in 1983 to 12 years in prison/exile for distributing anti-Soviet propaganda. (Begun had applied to leave Russia 12 years earlier, but his application was denied.)

October 15, 1987. Ida Nudel, a prisoner of Zion, arrives in Israel following 16 years of refused permission to leave Russia.

December 9, 1987. The Intifada, an organized Palestinian revolt against Israeli occupation of the Gaza Strip, begins. By the end of December, 21 Palestinians are dead and 179 wounded; 41 Israeli soldiers and 27 civilians are wounded.

March-April 1989. Abu Jihad, Arafat's military deputy, is killed in his Tunis home by commandos purported to be Israeli elite troops. Abu Jihad had masterminded an attack on a bus full of civilians (mostly mothers) in southern Israel and was guiding the Intifada revolt. (Israel has never claimed responsibility.)

July 6, 1989. Islamic Jihad terrorist forces Jerusalem-bound bus into a gorge, killing 16 and wounding 27.

July 27, 1989. Israeli commandos kidnap Hezbollah leader of south Lebanon, Sheikh Obeid, as a bargaining chip in negotiating the release of three Israeli soldiers held captive in Lebanon.

1989-1994. More than 500,000 Jewish immigrants reach Israel.

February 4, 1990. Nine Israeli tourists are killed and 17 wounded by Muslim fundamentalists in a tourist bus on the way to Cairo.

May 1, 1990. ~~Jewish Agency records record number of Russian Jews~~ leaving the USSR.

August 2, 1990. Iraq invades Kuwait and Israel distributes gas masks to all citizens.

September 8, 1990. Muslim fears that Jews are rebuilding the Third Temple lead to a riot in which thousands of Arabs attack an Israeli police station and beat officers. Twenty-six Jews are injured, 140 Arabs are injured and 21 Arabs are killed.

December 12, 1990. The USSR and Israel restore diplomatic ties.

January 17, 1991. Saddam Hussein fires 8 Scud missiles into Israel, causing much damage. In all, 39 Scuds are fired. More than 9,000 apartments and hundreds of businesses are damaged, 300 people slightly injured; 1 killed. Israel assents to American requests not to respond. On February 25 a cease-fire is declared.

May 25, 1991. Operation Solomon brings 14,000 Ethiopian followers of Judaism to Israel in 40 airlifts within 35 hours.

October 30, 1991. The Madrid International Middle East Peace Committee meets, discussing "land for peace."

January 24, 1992. Israel and China establish full diplomatic relations

March 1992. The Islamic Jihad bombs the Israeli Embassy in Argentina, killing 22 and injuring 252.

June 23, 1992. Yitshak Rabin wins election, defeating Yitzhak Shamir

September 13, 1993. Oslo Accords signed between the PLO and Israel, with U.S. support. This accord is understood as promoting land for peace and expressing the PLO's desire to solve disputes in a peaceful manner. Forty-thousand Israelis demonstrate for the accord, 50,000 against it.

October 14, 1993. First McDonald's restaurant opens in Israel, in Ramat Gan.

February 25, 1994. Baruch Goldstein kills 29 Muslims and wounds 100 in an attack on a Muslim service in Hebron's Machpelah Cave, on Purim, the Feast of Esther. Two of his friends had been murdered on December 6 by terrorists.

June 12, 1994. Lubavitch Rabbi Menachem Schneerson, head of the Chabad Hasidic stream, dies at age 92. Many of his followers believed that he was the messiah and would be resurrected.

July 1, 1994. Arafat arrives to cheering crowds in Gaza and later in Jericho.

July 18, 1994. Terrorists detonate a car bomb, blowing up the Jewish community center in Buenos Aires, Argentina. Thirty-seven are killed and 59 are missing.

July 26, 1994. Terrorists detonate a car bomb at the Israeli Embassy in London, injuring 13.

October 19, 1994. A Hamas suicide bomber blows up a Tel Aviv bus, killing 22 and injuring 44.

October 26, 1994. Israel and Jordan sign a peace treaty.

January 22, 1995. Two Islamic Jihad suicide bombers blow themselves up at Beit Lid junction, killing 21 and injuring 34.

July 24, 1995. Seven are killed and 32 injured by a suicide bus bomber in Tel Aviv.

August 21, 1995. ~~Five are killed and 107 injured in Jerusalem suicide~~ bus bombing. Both bombs were built by Yihye Ayash, the "Engineer."

October 25, 1995. Fathi Shkaki, one of Islamic Jihad's leaders, is killed by gunmen in Malta.

November 4, 1995. Prime Minister Yitzhak Rabin is assassinated by Yigal Amir, a 26-year-old law student and opponent of the Oslo Accords.

January 5, 1996. The "Engineer" is killed by a booby-trapped cell phone in Gaza.

February 25, 1996. Twenty-seven are killed and 78 injured by two suicide bombs in Jerusalem and Ashkelon.

March 3, 1996. Eighteen are killed and dozens injured by a suicide bus bomb in Jerusalem.

March 4, 1996. Fourteen are killed and 157 injured by a suicide bomb at Dizengoff Center, Tel Aviv, on the Feast of Purim.

May 29, 1996. Binyamin Netanyahu becomes Prime Minister of Israel.

September 24, 1996. An archeological tunnel along the Western Wall opens in Jerusalem. Rioting by Muslims spreads with tens of thousands attacking Israeli forces. Forty-one Israeli soldiers and 69 Palestinians are killed.

January 15, 1997. Israel redeploys in Hebron, according to the Oslo Accords.

March 13, 1997. A Jordanian soldier kills seven eighth-grade schoolgirls on the Island of Peace, between Jordan and Israel on the Jordan River.

July 30, 1997. Thirteen are killed and 120 injured by Hamas suicide bombers in Jerusalem.

1998-2000. Israeli forces withdraw from all major West Bank and Gaza cities (98 percent of Arab West Bank population). The Al Aqsa Intifad begins on the Feast of Trumpets 2000.

Author's Note: This overview of Israeli history was developed from information compiled and provided by Avner Boskey and from invaluable information appearing in Derek Princes' book, *The Last Word On the Middle East* (Lincoln, VA: Chosen Books, 1982), pp. 143-153.

OVERVIEW OF RUSSIAN HISTORY

700-500 BC. Jewish exiles establish communities in Armenia and Georgia.

AD 100. The first Jewish settlements on the northern shores of the Black Sea near Sevastopol are established.

700. The Khazar empire converts to Judaism and settles in the area of Kiev.

980. Vladimir, prince of Kiev, converts to Greek Orthodox Christianity.

1200. Moscow eclipses Kiev as the capital of Russia.

1550. Tsar Ivan IV orders all Jews in Pskov to convert or be drowned.

1648. Polish Jews massacred in Chmielnitski, Ukraine.

1727. Jews banished from many areas of Russia.

1742. Tsarina Elizabeth Petrovna expels any remaining Russian Jews. "I do not want any benefit from the enemies of Christ," she said.

1796. Catherine II (the Great) conquers Poland. Most of Eastern Europe's Jews are now under Russian rule.

1791-1815. Pale of Settlement, a specific area to which Jews are limited by tsarist decree, is established.

1817. Tsar Alexander I outlaws so-called "blood libel" against the Jewish population.

1805-1822. The systematic expulsion of Jewish people from Russian and Belorussian villages is under way.

1825-1855. Nicholas I orders the forced conscription of all Jewish males from 12 to 25 years of age into the Russian army. The goal is to assimilate all Jews.

1844. Jewish people are forced into Russian schools, with the secret purpose to destroy Jewish life and Judaism. Wearing Jewish traditional clothes and sidecurls is declared illegal.

1881-1894. Tsar Alexander institutes the Anti-Jewish Temporary Laws of May 1882.

1881-1906. Government-sponsored mobs attack Jews (looting, murdering and raping) in Kiev, Kirovograd, Balta, Dnepropetrovsk, Krivio Rog, Nizhni Novgorod, Kishinev, Zhitomer, Mialystok and Siedlce.

1884. K. Pobedonostev, head of the Russian Orthodox Church's Holy Synod, states the government objectives regarding the Jewish people: "One-third of the Jews will convert, one-third will die and one-third will flee the country."

1881-1914. More than 2 million Jews leave Russia, most go to North America.

1900. A forgery by tsarist secret police titled *Protocols of the Elders of Zion* is published. It gives the details of a supposed Jewish plot for world domination. This fabrication is still promulgated by neo-Nazi and Islamic groups today.

1911. In the "blood libel" trial in Kiev, Mendel Beilis is accused of slaughtering Christian children and using their blood in Jewish rituals.

1913. Joseph Stalin authors *Marxism and the National Question*, which presents a Bolshevik solution to the "Jewish Question": The Jews are not a real nation; therefore, they are not entitled to a homeland.

1917-1921. The Soviet Period begins. The Soviet Civil War erupts. Bread riots and strikes take place in Petrograd. Jews are attacked and slaughtered by both Communist Reds and tsarist Whites, starting in Ukraine in 1918. More than 530 communities are attacked, more than 60,000 people are murdered, and more than 200,000 people are wounded.

February 1917. The first Russian Revolution takes place. Tsar Nicholas II is deposed. Kerensky comes to power. Kamenev and Stalin return from Siberia.

April 1917. Lenin returns to Russia. Lenin's *April Theses* is published. The Coalition Provisional Government is formed. Russia launches a campaign against Germans.

October 1917. The second Russian Revolution takes place. Kerensky is deposed. The Bolsheviks come to power.

1918-1923. The *Yevsektzia* (Jewish section of the Communist party) is established, which systematically destroys Judaism, Hebrew and Zionist activities.

January 1918. The Constituent Assembly is dissolved.

February 1918. Separation of church and state is established. Russia moves to the Gregorian Calendar.

March 3, 1918. The Treaty of Brest-Litovsk is signed. The Seventh Party Congress convenes. British troops land at Murmansk.

April 1918. Japanese troops land at Vladivostok.

June 1918. Committees of the Village Poor are established. Industry is nationalized.

July 10, 1918. Intervention begins. The Lenin (RFSFR) Constitution is ratified.

July 17, 1918. Tsar Nicholas II and his family are murdered.

August 1918. American troops land in Vladivostok.

September 1918. American troops land at Archangelsk.

November 1918. World War I ends. The Soviets repudiate the Treaty of Brest-Litovsk. French troops land at Odessa.

December 1918. British troops land at Batum.

1919. The Comintern is founded.

March 1919. Kolchak launches a drive against Bolsheviks. The Eighth Party Congress convenes.

April 1919. French troops withdraw from Odessa.

June 28, 1919. The Treaty of Versailles is signed.

August 1919. All Jewish communities are dissolved and their property confiscated.

October 1919. Allied troops withdraw from Murmansk and Archangel.

January 1920. Kolchak is shot by Bolsheviks. The Allied blockade is lifted.

March 1920. The Ninth Party Congress convenes.

April 1920. Wrangel replaces Denikin.

November 1920. Wrangel evacuates Crimea. Civil War ends in Russia.

1921. The Kronstadt Uprising occurs. The Tenth Party Congress convenes and issues orders for "the purge." The Treaty of Riga with Poland is signed.

April 1922. Stalin becomes secretary general. The Treaty of Rapallo with Germany is signed. The Eleventh Party Congress convenes. Lenin suffers his first stroke. The USSR declares itself a nation.

December 23, 1922. Lenin begins his *Testament*.

1923. The Twelfth Party Congress convenes. Lenin suffers a second stroke.

January 4, 1923. Lenin finishes his *Testament*.

January 1924. Lenin dies from 4th stroke. Stalin overcomes Zinoviev, Kamenev and Trotsky by stirring up anti-Semitism against all three.

1924. The Thirteenth Party Congress convenes. The USSR's constitution is ratified. Petrograd is renamed Leningrad. The USSR is recognized by Great Britain, France and Italy.

1925. The Fourteenth Party Congress convenes. Trotsky is removed as war commissar.

1926. Trotsky, Zinoviev and Kamenev are ousted from the Politburo.

1927. The Fifteenth Party Congress convenes: Trotsky, Zinoviev and followers are expelled from the Communist party. Stalin takes control. The Communist revolt in China is crushed.

1928. The first Five-Year Plan is adopted. Birobidzhan, a Jewish settlement near the Chinese border, is established as a counterweight to Zionism.

1929. Trotsky is deported. Nikolai Bukharin is ousted from the Politburo. Collectivization and industrialization begin.

1930. The Sixteenth Party Congress convenes. Stalin delivers his "Dizzy with Success" speech. Government-sponsored anti-religious attacks target Judaism and Christianity.

1932-1933. The Ukrainian Famine strikes.

1932. The Russian Association of Proletarian Writers dissolves.

January 21, 1932. The Non-Aggression Pact with Finland is signed. "Socialist realism" is mentioned for the first time. A Soviet-French nonaggression pact is signed.

1933. The United States recognizes the USSR.

1933-1937. The second Five-Year Plan is approved.

May 7, 1934. Birobidzhan becomes an autonomous Jewish region.

1934. The Seventeenth Party Congress is convened. The Soviet Union joins the League of Nations. Kirov is assassinated. The Stalinist purges begin.

1936. Gorky dies. The Jewish socialist leadership of Birobidzhan (autonomous Jewish region) is liquidated.

December 1936. Stalin's constitution is promulgated. Show trials of Zinoviev, Kamenev and others are conducted.

1937-41. *Stalinshchina* (Stalin Terror) is launched.

1939. The Eighteenth Party Congress convenes. Minimum labor days are set for collective farms. Molotov and Von Ribbentrop sign the Soviet-German Anti-Aggression Pact. Poland's Jews come under Nazi and Communist control. World War II: Germany invades Poland. The Soviets occupy Estonia, Latvia and Lithuania. Stalin is named Man of the Year by *TIME*. There are Soviet attacks on Poland and Finland.

1940. Was with Finland ends. The Baltic states are annexed. Trotsky is murdered in Mexico.

1941. Germans invade the USSR. Stalin names himself as head of the government.

September 1, 1941. Mass evacuation of Volga Germans is held.

1941-1945. Marks the beginning of the systematic slaughter of Eastern European Jewry. Few are evacuated by Soviet forces.

1942. Churchill visits Moscow. Stalin is named Man of the Year by *TIME* again. Nazis invade the Soviet Union. The Jewish Anti-Fascist Committee is established to garner Western Jewish support for the Soviet Union.

1943. German troops surrender at Stalingrad. The Comintern is dissolved. Sergius becomes patriarch. The Moscow Conference and the Teheran Conference are held.

May 11, 1944. Crimean Tatars are banished to Siberia.

February 1945. The Yalta Conference convenes.

July-Aug. 1945. Vienna and Berlin are taken by Russian troops. The Potsdam Conference is held.

July 24, 1945. The U.S. successfully tests an atom bomb.

1946. The first elections are held for Supreme Soviet since 1937. Churchill delivers his "Sinews of Peace" speech at Westminster College. Eisenstein's *Ivan the Terrible, Part II*, is withdrawn from theaters. The first session of the United Nations opens. Communists come into power in Bulgaria.

1947. Rationing is abolished. Cominform is established.

1948. Solomon Michoels, chairman of the Jewish Anti-Fascist Committee, is murdered by the secret police in Minsk. Twenty-five top leaders subsequently are arrested and secretly executed on August 12, 1952, on charges of treason, including an alleged plan to establish a Jewish state in Crimea. Czechoslovakia joins the Soviet bloc. The Berlin blockade occurs. Yugoslavia is expelled from Cominform.

1949. The USSR tests the atomic bomb.

1950. The USSR and China sign an alliance treaty.

1952. The Prague Trials are held; many Jews are charged and executed for "Zionism and other crimes against the State."

1953. "The Doctor's Plot," a charge that a group of Jewish Kremlin doctors were conspiring to poison Stalin and other top officials, leads to charges of Russia-wide Jewish conspiracies, a show trial and plans for a mass deportation of Russia's Jews to the distant east. This ends with Stalins's death. Malenkov is named premier, Khrushchev, first secretary. Beria is executed.

1954. Crimea is transferred to Ukraine.

1954-1956. Khrushchev's announces his Virgin Land program.

1955. Malenkov is replaced by Bulganin. The Summit Conference is held in Geneva. The Warsaw Pact is established.

1956. Khrushchev delivers his "Secret Speech." Lenin's *Testament* is read. The party condemns the "cult of the individual." The Hungarian Revolution is quashed. Molotov resigns.

1957. Malenkov, Kaganovich and Molotov are ousted. The economy is decentralized. The First Sputnik is launched. The USSR successfully tests ICBM.

1958. Bulganin resigns. Boris Pasternak is awarded the Nobel Prize for literature.

1959. Mikoyan, Kozlov and Khrushchev visit the U.S. Khrushchev launches his corn campaign. The Twenty-First Party Congress convenes. "Anti-Party Group" is denounced.

1959-1960. Systematic arrests and executions are made of those guilty of economic crimes (free enterprise). So high was the number of Jews arrested and executed that the International Commission of Jurists in Geneva stated that Jews were being targeted as scapegoats for economic unrest.

1960. Khrushchev visits the UN Assembly in New York. Boris Pasternak dies.

1961. Yurii Gagarin becomes the first man in space. The Twenty-Second

Party Congress convenes and announces a new program and rules. Stalin's remains are removed from the Lenin Mausoleum. The Berlin Wall is built.

1962. Solzhenitsyn's *One Day in the Life of Ivan Denisovich* is published. The October Cuban Missile Crisis occurs.

1963. The Russian-Chinese split deepens. The U.S.-USSR hot line is established. The U.S., the USSR and Great Britain sign a nuclear test ban treaty. Khrushchev is ousted. Kosygin becomes premier.

1965. Demonstrations occur in Moscow against U.S. air raids in North Vietnam. Mikhail Sholokhov wins the Nobel Prize in literature.

1967. The Outer Space Treaty is signed. Svetlana Alliluyeva, Stalin's daughter, defects. Andropov becomes head of the KGB.

1968. The Soviets invade Czechoslovakia. The dissident (*inakomyshlyashchii*) movement begins.

Israel's Six-Day War victory leads to a resurgence of Jewish activism focused on immigration to Israel and protest against anti-Jewish activities. A swell of anti-Israeli and anti-Jewish publications and expressions rises in the USSR, comparing Jews to Nazis and characterizing Zionism as the worst enemy of mankind.

1969. Preliminary round of SALT talks is held.

1970. The U.S.-Soviet Treaty on the Non-Proliferation of Nuclear Weapons is ratified. Alexander Solzhenitsyn wins the Nobel Prize for literature.

1970-1971. The SALT talks progress. In Leningrad, 11 Jews attempt to hijack a Russian Israel-bound plane. They are given harsh sentences, including two death sentences (subsequently cancelled after worldwide pressure).

1971. Khrushchev dies. Solzhenitsyn is deported from the USSR. The Twenty-Fourth Party Congress convenes. Jews are forced to pay an exit tax to leave Russia.

1972. U.S. President Richard Nixon travels to Moscow for a summit. The SALT Treaty is signed. SALT II negotiations begin.

1974. Solzhenitsyn is expelled to West Germany. The third Moscow summit is held.

1975. The Apollo-Soyuz Mission is launched. Sakharov wins the Nobel Prize for peace, but a visa to attend ceremonies is denied.

1977. Dissidents Ginzburg, Rudenko, Orlov and Shcharinskii are arrested. The Brezhnev Constitution is ratified.

1978. The Soviet UN Undersecretary for Political and Security Council Affairs defects to U.S. Solzhenytsin delivers his Harvard speech.

1979. Gorbachev is made a candidate member of the Politburo. The Soviets invade Afghanistan.

1980. A U.S. grain embargo is launched to protest the invasion of Afghanistan. Sakharov is exiled. Sixty-four countries boycott the Moscow Summer Olympics to protest the Soviet invasion of Afghanistan. Gorbachev is promoted to a full member of the Politburo.

1982. Andropov is promoted to secretariat. Brezhnev dies. Andropov becomes general secretary.

1983. A Korean airliner is shot down by the Soviets.

1984. Andropov dies. Chernenko becomes general secretary. The Soviets withdraw from the Summer Olympics in Los Angeles. Tarkovsky emigrates to Italy.

1985. Chernenko dies. Gorbachev becomes general secretary. Gorbachev calls for economic reforms (Perestroika).

1986. The Chernobyl disaster happens. A U.S.-Soviet summit is held in Reykjavik, Iceland, between President Ronald Reagan and Gorbachev. Gorbachev starts an anticorruption campaign.

1987. Sakharov is freed after seven years of exile in Gorky. Mikhail Gorbachev is named *TIME* Man of the Year. Gorbachev sets 1991 as the deadline for an overhaul of the economy. Soviet diplomats go to Israel for first official visit since 1967. A U.S.-Soviet summit is held in Washington, D.C.

1988. There is ethnic unrest in the Baltic republics. Soviets begin to pull out of Afghanistan. The U.S. and the USSR have a summit in Moscow. Gorbachev becomes president. Gorbachev gives a speech at the UN, announcing significant cuts in Soviet military strength.

1989. Soviets complete their pullout from Afghanistan. The first multi-candidate elections are held and several uncontested candidates are defeated. Yeltsin and Sakharov overwhelmingly win seats in the Congress of People's Deputies. Protesters in Georgia demand independence. Soviet troops move in purging of "dead souls" in the Central Committee. Coal miners strike in Siberia, Ukraine and Central Asia. Demonstrators in the Baltics want independence. RUKH (Popular Movement of the Ukraine) demands independence. The Congress of People's Deputies of the USSR begins political reforms. Azerbaijani Popular Front imposes blockade on 85 percent of freight entering Armenia. Armenia and Azerbaijani engage in a civil war. The Berlin Wall comes down. Andrei Sakharov dies.

1990. Mikhail Gorbachev is awarded the Nobel Prize for peace. Russia's first McDonald's opens on Gorky Street. Elections are held for regional deputies of the Russian Federation. Lithuania declares independence. Yeltsin announces his resignation from the Communist party. The Supreme Soviet passes a law to lift censorship from the press. Congress of Peoples Deputies of RSFSR passes the Declaration of State Sovereignty of Russia (Independence Day). A law on peasant farms allows *kolkhozniks* (people who had worked on collective farms) to own private farms. The CFE Treaty is signed in Paris.

1991. The Soviet army attacks public buildings in Riga and Vilnius. Boris Yeltsin becomes first democratically elected Russian President. The bodies of Nicholas II and family are exhumed.

August 1991. Yanayev, Pugo, Yazov and three others announce a takeover. Yeltsin speaks to the crowd from a tank then barricades himself in the Parliament building. Latvia declares its independence. Gorbachev returns from house arrest in Crimea. Pugo commits suicide. Gorbachev resigns as head of Communist party. Yeltsin closes *Pravda* and disbands the Communist party.

APPENDIX 3

DATES OF PURIM AND THE ESTHER FAST

BY JIM GOLL WITH ED AND BEV DANIELS

Purim is a Jewish holiday observed in celebration of God's supernatural deliverance of the Jewish people from Haman's genocidal plot to destroy them in the time of Persia's King Artaxerxes. The holiday was held the 14th of Adar (according to the Jewish calendar) in the unwalled cities and the 15th of Adar in the cities that were walled in the time of Joshua.

Esther called for a nationwide three-day fast preceding her intervention on behalf of the Jewish people. She entered the royal throne room on the third day (see Esther 4:16—5:1). This is the same fast we call for the Church, the spiritual Esther, to intercede once again on behalf of the Jewish people for deliverance from Haman's plot.

Year	Feast of Purim	Esther Fast Dates
2002	February 26	February 24-26
2003	March 18	March 16-18
2004	March 7	March 5-7
2005	March 25	March 23-25
2006	March 14	March 12-14
2007	March 4	March 2-4
2008	March 21	March 19-21
2009	March 10	March 8-10
2010	February 28	February 26-28

2011	March 20	March 18-20
2012	March 8	March 6-8
2013	February 24	February 22-24
2014	March 16	March 14-16
2015	March 5	March 3-5
2016	March 24	March 22-24
2017	March 12	March 10-12
2018	March 1	February 27-March 1
2019	March 21	March 19-21
2020	March 10	March 8-10

BIBLE REFERENCES

Prophecies of God's Word:

Genesis 12:1-3; 35:11-12; Jeremiah 23:3-7; 30:10; Ezekiel 20:33-35; 36:17-28; Zephaniah 2:1-2.

Performance of God's Word:

Isaiah 49:22; 59:21; Jeremiah 31:37; Ezekiel 36; Romans 11:11,12; 17,18,25-31; 15:27; Ephesians 3:6.

General References for Further Study:

Deuteronomy 4:27; 28:64a; 30:1-4; 32:26.

Psalm 105:37,42,43; 106:44-47; 122:6; 137:4-6; 147:1,2.

Isaiah 11:10-12; 14:1,2; 27:12,13; 36:8-10; 40:1-5; 41:8-11; 42:22; 43:1,2,6,8,13; 44:3-6; 45:2-6; 46:3,4; 49:8-10; 51:14; 57: 18;41; 60:4,8,9; 62:4-7,10-12.

Jeremiah 13:16-18; 16:14-16, 23:3,7,8; 30:16,17; 31:7-11,31-34.

Ezekiel 34:11-13,16; 36:8,24-28; 37:12-14; 39:27,28.

Hosea, chapters 3,4,11,14.

Amos 9:11-14.

Micah 4:6,7.

Zephaniah 2:6,7.
Romans 15:27.

INSTRUCTIONS FOR PRAYER AND FASTING

1. During the days of the fast, eat or drink absolutely nothing. The only exception is the taking of the Holy Communion.

2. If you are not experienced with fasting, it is a good idea to start with one-day fasts the month before you attempt the Esther Fast.

3. You should not fast if you are pregnant or suffering from illness or some other medical condition.

4. When you complete your fast, come off it gradually. Do not eat meat for the first day and a half after your fast. When you begin to eat, consume light foods such as juices, soup, bread and crackers. Gradually add more protein foods until you are eating normally again at the end of the second day.

5. Be sure to spend extra time praying and reading the Scriptures. This is the purpose of fasting: so that you can devote yourself without reservation to seeking God in prayer. Study the verses given at the end of chapter 5 that deal with Israel's return to the Land.

6. Be specific in your prayers. You can refer to the Prayer for the Oppressed Jews found in chapter 3 and the list of items for prayer given in the Esther Fast Mandate in chapter 8. You could also contact your Christian friends who are fasting and exchange prayer requests with them. The following is a brief outline of some categories in which to pray:

> **Pray** for forgiveness for yourself and also for the sins of your nation as Daniel did (see chapter 9).
> **Pray** for God's direction in your life and ministry.
> **Pray** for reconciliation in your own personal relationships as well as among groups, regions and nations.
> **Pray** specifically about your own ministry in the Body of

Christ. Ask God to direct and empower you so that you may be a blessing using the ministry gifts He has given you.

Pray so as to deepen your commitment as you yield yourself to the Lord in every area of your life.

PRAYER POINTS FOR "THE CRY"

BY JIM W. GOLL WITH AVNER BOSKEY

The material in this section is adapted from appendix 2: "Scriptures for Praying for Israel" in my book *Kneeling on the Promises* (Jim Goll. Grand Rapids, MI: Chosen Books, 1999), and is used by permission. For another excellent complementary tool in intercession, listen to my *Prayers For Israel* (available in CD or audiocassette). These effective tools are available at www.mttnweb.com and www.jimgoll.com.

1. SCRIPTURES AND SENTIMENTS TO PRAY FOR ISRAEL

A. Foundational Scriptures on Israel's future

1. Hosea 1:10: Yet the number of the sons of Israel will be like the sand of the sea, which cannot be measured or numbered; and in the place where it is said to them, "You are not My people," it will be said to them, "You are the sons of the living God."

2. Jeremiah 31:8-10: "Behold, I am bringing them from the north country, and I will gather them from the remote parts of the earth, among them the blind and the lame, the woman with child and she who is in labor with child, together; a great company, they shall return here. With weeping they shall come, and by supplication I will lead them; I will make them walk by streams of waters, on a straight path in which they will not stumble; for I am a father to Israel, and Ephraim is My firstborn." Hear the

word of the LORD, O nations, and declare in the coast-
lands afar off, and say, "He who scattered Israel will
gather him and keep him as a shepherd keeps his flock."

B. More Scriptures and observations on aliyah, the return to
the land

1. Jeremiah 16:14,15: "Therefore behold, days are coming,"
declares the LORD, "when it will no longer be said, 'As
the LORD lives, who brought up the sons of Israel out of
the land of Egypt,' but, 'As the LORD lives, who brought up
the sons of Israel from the land of the north and from all the
countries where He had banished them.' For I will restore
them to their own land which I gave to their fathers."

2. Jeremiah 23:7,8: "Therefore behold, the days are coming,"
declares the LORD, "when they will no longer say, 'As the
LORD lives, who brought up the sons of Israel from the
land of Egypt,' but, 'As the LORD lives, who brought up
and led back the descendants of the household of Israel
from the north land and from all the countries where I
had driven them.' Then they will live on their own soil."

3. Isaiah 11:11,12: Then it will happen on that day that the
Lord will again recover the second time with His hand
the remnant of His people, who will remain, from
Assyria, Egypt, Pathros, Cush, Elam, Shinar, Hamath,
and from the islands of the sea. And He will lift up a
standard for the nations and assemble the banished
ones of Israel, and will gather the dispersed of Judah
from the four corners of the earth.

4. Isaiah 43:5,6: Do not fear, for I am with you; I will bring
your offspring from the east, and gather you from the
west. I will say to the north, "Give them up!" And to the
south, "Do not hold them back." Bring My sons from
afar and My daughters from the ends of the earth.

5. In June 2000, Israel celebrated the immigration of the 1 millionth Russian-speaking from the Land of the North. Russian is now the second leading spoken language in Israel! May more come forth in Jesus name!

C. Our scriptural response

1. Jeremiah 30:3: "For behold, days are coming," declares the Lord, "when I will restore the fortunes of My people Israel and Judah." The LORD says, "I will also bring them back to the land that I gave to their forefathers and they shall possess it."

2. Jeremiah 31:7: For thus says the LORD, "Sing aloud with gladness for Jacob, and shout among the chief of the nations; proclaim, give praise, and say, 'O LORD, save Your people, the remnant of Israel.'"

3. The three keys are to *proclaim*, to *praise* and to *pray*. These are our clear biblical mandates.

II. EIGHT BIBLICAL INTERCESSORY PRAYERS FOR ISRAEL

A. From the life of Moses

1. Exodus 32:11-13,32. Moses' cry to the Lord based on the Hebrews reputation and His in the earth, and on His covenant, as well as for His glory's sake.

2. Deuteronomy 9:18,19, 25-29. Moses' fasting for 40 days for intervention in a time of great crisis.

3. Numbers 14:13-19: But now, I pray, let the power of the Lord be great (v. 17). (This is followed by an intense cry for pardon according to God's great loving-kindness.)

B. From the life of Solomon

1. 1 Kings 8:46-53. A simple prayer for God to forgive as He has done before.
2. Deuteronomy 30:1-10. The proclamation of restoration as taught to the sons.

C. From the life of Nehemiah

Nehemiah. 1:4-11. The compassionate plea before God for the forgiveness of His people.

D. From the life of Asaph and the sons of Korah

1. Psalm 44: Rise up, be our help . . . redeem us! (v. 26).
2. Psalm 74. An appeal against the devastation of the land by the enemy.
3. Psalm 79. A lament over the destruction of Jerusalem and a cry for help.
4. Psalm 80: Save us! Restore us! Revive us! (vv. 2,3,18).
5. Psalm 83. A prayer for the Lord to confound their enemies.
6. Psalm 85. A prayer for God's mercy upon the nation.
7. Psalm 123: Be gracious to us, O Lord, be gracious to us (v. 3).

E. From the life of Joel

1. Joel 1:8,13,14. A call to a solemn assembly.
2. Joel 2:12-17. An intercessory cry to "Spare Your people, O Lord."

F. From the life of Isaiah

1. Isaiah 63:15—64:12. A desperate prayer for mercy and help.

2. Isaiah 58:1: Cry loudly, do not hold back.

3. Isaiah 62:1,6: For Zion's sake I will not keep silent, and for Jerusalem's sake I will not keep quiet. . . . All day and all night they will never keep silent.

G. From the life of Jeremiah

1. Jeremiah 14:7-9,17-22: O LORD, act for Your name's sake! Truly our apostasies have been many, we have sinned against You (vv. 7-9).

2. Jeremiah 15:5. A plea in the midst of judgment.

3. Jeremiah 9:1: That I might weep day and night.

4. Lamentations 3:43-51: My eyes pour down unceasingly, without stopping, until the LORD looks down and sees from heaven (vv. 49,50).

5. Lamentations 5:19-22: Restore us to Your, O LORD, that we may be restored (v. 21).

H. From the life of Daniel

1. Daniel 6:10. The example of "Kneeling on the Promises" three times each day.

2. Daniel 9:1-19: O Lord hear! O Lord forgive! O Lord, listen and take action! For Your own sake, O my God, do not delay, because Your city and Your people are called by Your name (v. 19). Daniel's prayer of confession on behalf of his people (our biblical model to follow today).

III. SEVEN REASONS WHY I SHOULD PRAY FOR ISRAEL

A. Israel is still the apple of God's eye and His inheritance, close to His heart.

1. Psalm 148:14: And He has lifted up a horn for His people, Praise for all His godly ones; even for the sons of Israel, a people near to Him.

2. Zechariah 2:8: He who touches you, touches the apple of His eye.

3. Deuteronomy 32:8-11: the LORD's portion is His people; Jacob is the allotment of His inheritance. . . . He encircled him, He cared for him, He guarded him as the pupil of His eye. . . . He spread His wings and caught them, He carried them on His pinions (v. 9-11).

4. Romans 11:29: For the gifts and the calling of God are irrevocable.

5. Psalm 33:11,12: The plans of His heart [proceed] from generation to generation (v. 11).

B. God says that His servants should pray with compassion over Israel's condition. Psalm 102:13-17: You will arise and have compassion on Zion; for it is time to be gracious to her, for the appointed time has come. Surely Your servants find pleasure in her stones and feel pity for her dust (vv. 13-14).

C. Pray until God commands us to give Him and ourselves no rest until He establishes Jerusalem and makes her the praise of the earth. Isaiah 62:1,6,7: For Zion's sake I will not keep silent, and for Jerusalem's sake I will not keep quiet, until her righteousness goes forth like brightness, and her salvation like a torch that is burning. . . . On your walls, O Jerusalem, I have appointed watchmen; all day and all night they will never keep silent. You who remind the LORD, take no rest for yourselves; and give Him no rest until He establishes and makes Jerusalem a praise in the earth.

D. Receive God's heart. God's heart will travail through us for Israel's salvation.

   1. Romans 9:2,3: I [Paul] have great sorrow and unceasing grief in my heart (v. 2).
   2. Romans 10:1,14: My prayer to God for them is for their salvation (v. 1).

E. Seek spiritual and physical well being. God commands us to seek the spiritual and physical good of the Israeli people and to pray for the peace of Jerusalem.

   1. Psalm 122:4,6-9: To which the tribes go up, even the tribes of the LORD—an ordinance for Israel. . . . Pray for the peace of Jerusalem: "May they prosper who love you. May peace be within your walls, and prosperity within your palaces" (vv. 4,6).
   2. Romans 15:25-27: But now, I am going to Jerusalem serving the saints. For Macedonia and Achaia have been pleased to make a contribution for the poor among the saints in Jerusalem. Yes, they were pleased to do so, and they are indebted to them. For if the Gentiles have shared in their spiritual things, they are indebted to minister to them also in material things.
   3. Romans 1:16: For I am not ashamed of the gospel, for it is the power of God for salvation to everyone who believes, to the Jew first and also to the Greek.
   4. Romans 2:9-11: Tribulation and distress . . . glory and honor and peace . . . to the Jew first . . . there is no partiality with God.

F. The Jewish people's acceptance of Messiah Jesus will lead to life from the dead—world-wide revival of unprecedented magnitude.

1. Romans 11:15: For if their rejection be the reconciliation of the world, what will their acceptance be but life
   from the dead?

2. Isaiah 27:6: In the days to come Jacob will take root,
   Israel will blossom and sprout, and they will fill the
   whole world with fruit.

G. His Second Coming. Jesus linked His Second Coming to
   Israel's national turning to Him. May it be so! Matthew
   23:39: "For I say to you, from now on you shall not see Me
   until you say, 'Blessed is He who comes in the name of the
   Lord!'"

IV. CLOSING PRACTICAL PRAYER
AND ACTION POINTS

A. Acts of Identificational Repentance

> Cry out to the Lord with brokenness that our Father
> would forgive us, the Church, for our apathy and
> fear and for not speaking up and acting with right-
> eousness in past times of history. (For more details
> see chapter 7 of my book *Father Forgive Us*, which is
> listed in the recommended reading at the end of
> this book.)

B. Prayer for an Awakening

> Ask the Lord to awaken the global Church of Jesus
> Christ in this hour to the immediacy and urgency of
> this message. Intercede that the Lord would raise up
> modern-day Esthers, Josephs, Daniels and Debras
> "for such a time as this."

C. Prayer for an Extension of Time

Pray for an extension of a time of mercy and freedom so that the Russian Jews may flee during a time of safety so that the time of the fishers could continue.

D. Prayer for Protection

Pray for the protection of Russian Jews as we possibly transition from the time of the fishers into the time of the hunters. Pray and prepare for places of safety and refuge to be raised up for times of persecution of the Jewish people. Intercede that the enemy's plans would be thwarted and that God's destiny for the Jewish people would be fulfilled in this generation.

E. Prayer for a Movement of Signs and Wonders

Petition the Lord to release an increase of His presence with a movement of signs and wonders. Pray that the blinders would fall off the eyes of the Jewish people and that they would recognize and receive Jesus Christ as their sovereign Lord.

Referral Ministries

A number of ministries have demonstrated a genuine heart for Israel over the years. If you want to help the Jewish people make aliyah from the Land of the North and from other places around the world, please contact the ministries listed below for more information.

Caleb Company, The
Don Finto
68 Music Square East
Nashville, TN 37203
(615) 256-2123
Internet: www.calebcompany.com
E-mail: donfinto@compuserve.com

Don Finto is the former senior pastor of Belmont Church in Nashville. He now directs the Caleb Company, a ministry that encourages a love for the Jewish people and the land of Israel.

Derek Prince Ministries
DPM-USA
1800 E. Associates Lane
Charlotte, NC 28217-2801
(704) 357-3556
Internet: www.derekprince.com
E-mail: ContactUs@us.derekprince.com

This is the ministry office of Bible teacher and author Derek Prince. More information about his support of Israel and about how to obtain his books can be obtained at his website.

Ebenezer House
>   5a Poole Road
>   Bournemouth BH2 5QJ, England
>   E-mail: ecf@btinternet.com

The ministry raises funds to help Jewish people make aliyah by ship and by airplane from the Land of the North and around the world. It was founded by Gustav Scheller and Johannes Facius.

Embrace Israel Ministries
>   Reuven Doron
>   P.O. Box 10077
>   Cedar Rapids, IA 52410-0077
>   Internet: www.embraceisrael.org
>   E-mail: mailbox@embraceisrael.org

Doron lives in Jerusalem and provides valuable information and prayer guidance for those around the world who love Israel. He does this by sending his bimonthly newsletter, *Prayer Focus from Jerusalem,* to select groups of intercessors worldwide.

Exobus Project
>   P.O. Box 1030
>   Hull HU3 2YG, England
>   E-mail: exobus@exobus.org

This ministry operates a fleet of buses with a staff of volunteers from many different countries. They work tirelessly to help transport Jewish people making aliyah from their homes in other countries to major airports, ports or transportation hubs where other transportation awaits them. It is difficult, if not impossible, at times for these immigrants to make their way from rural areas to these major transportation points in the Land of the North or in other areas where hostility is often shown toward Jewish people.

Final Frontier Ministries

Avner and Rachel Boskey

P.O. Box 1721

Antioch, TN 37011-1721

Internet: www.jimgoll.com/a_boskey.htm

E-mail: psalm67@netvision.net.il

Avner Boskey has served the Jewish people of the Land of the North as a pastor and a planter of Messianic congregations. He also leads prayer tours to Israel.

Harvest Bibles

Richard Glickstein

P.O. Box 434

Hermitage, TN 37076-0434

Internet: www.harvestchristian.com

Harvest Bibles provides Russian-language New Testaments to Jews in the former Soviet Union. For more details, see page 253 this book.

Hear O Israel Ministries

Jonathan Bernis

P.O. Box 30990

Phoenix, AZ 85046-0408

E-mail: HOIM@compuserve.com

Bernis conducts powerful Messianic Jewish music festivals around the world to introduce Jewish people and Gentiles to the Messiah. This ministry offers incredible opportunities for volunteers to help conduct these outreach festivals.

International Fellowship of Christians and Jews
Rabbi Yechiel Eckstein
309 W. Washington, Suite 800
Chicago, IL 60606-3200
Internet: www.ifcj.org
E-mail: ifcj@ifcg.org

Rabbi Eckstein's ministry helps transport Jewish people making *aliyah* to Israel from countries around the world. It also helps these new immigrants overcome the often difficult obstacles they face in Israel, where resources, housing and job opportunities are often limited and the barriers of language, culture and religious background can seem insurmountable.

Issachar International
David Fitzpatrick
P.O. Box 3561
Brentwood, TN 37024-3561
(615) 799-1385
Internet: www.pilgrimimages.com

David Fitzpatrick is a pastor, author and prophetic intercessor who has lived in Russia. He has a heart for God's purposes among the Jewish people. Fitzpatrick is the photographer who captured the images in this book. Copies of these images can be purchased directly from Fitzpatrick.

Jerusalem House of Prayer for All Nations

Tom Hess
P.O. Box 31393
91313 Jerusalem, Israel
E-mail: jhopfan@compuserve.com

Hess helps set up prayer watches around the world to pray for Israel and the Jewish people (as well as for local churches, cities and nations); and he conducts prayer convocations in Jerusalem and prayer pilgrimages in Israel.

Joseph Storehouse (Vision for Israel)

The Remnant of Israel (Barry Segal)
P.O. Box 16447
Savannah, GA 31416
Internet: www.remnantofisrael.com
E-mail: info@visionforisrael.com

Vision for Israel was established to help rebuild the nation of Israel, both spiritually and physically. The Joseph Storehouse is part of the ministry; it supplies humanitarian aid to Jewish people, Arabs and Messianic Christians in the Promised Land.

Messianic Vision

Sid Roth
P.O. Box 1918
Brunswick, GA 31521
(912) 265-2500
Internet: www.sidroth.org
E-mail: info@sidroth.org

Sid Roth has an international radio and television ministry. He has been active in supporting and encouraging Messianic congregations in Russia.

Prayer Shield for Israel and the Jewish People
    c/o Grace Community
    4878 Lickton Pike
    Whites Creek, TN 37189
    (615) 876-7668
    Internet: www.nashvilleprayershield.com

This ministry is steered by a board of directors including many who are mentioned in this book. David E. Long is acting coordinator. The group seeks people who are willing to make a commitment of an hour a week to pray and worship the Lord with Israel in mind. Contact Prayer Shield for more information on how you can participate.

The Watchman International
    Lars Enarson
    P.O. Box 3670
    Pensacola, FL 32516-3670
    Internet: www.thewatchman.org

Lars Enarson is an author of publications designed to help believers celebrate the biblical Feasts of Israel, leads in calls for intercession for Israel and the Jewish people and directs a yearly Passover prayer convocation in Jerusalem.

ENDNOTES

Chapter 1

1. This was the external audible voice of God, not an internal impression or thought.
2. C. Peter Wagner, "A Word upon Entering the New Millennium/APOS-TOLIC COUNCIL OF PROPHETIC ELDERS/November 30, 1999" (document read at the World Congress on Intercession, Colorado Springs, CO, December 4, 1999), point one.
3. "Hoshea ben Nun," or "Hoshea, son of Nun," is the original name of the biblical leader we know best as Joshua, son of Nun; the man who took Moses' place and led Israel across the Jordan and into the Promised Land. Moses changed Hoshea's name when Hoshea became his personal assistant, or servant (see Num. 13:16).
4. A. S. Van Der Woude, gen. ed., "1. Egypt and the Hittite Realm in the Thirteenth Century B.C.," in *The World of the Bible: Bible Handbook,* (Grand Rapids, MI: Wm. B. Eerdmans Publishing Company, 1986), vol. 1, pp. 275, 276. Rameses was one of two storage cities built by Hebrew slaves under the rule of Rameses II (see Exod. 1:11). Evidently it served as Egypt's capital city for nearly 300 years and was the site of Pharaoh's royal residence, Pi-Ramesse. Current research identifies the ruins of Quantir as the site of Rameses instead of the cities of Tanis or Zoan. [From "Rameses" in *The Holman Bible Dictionary* (Nashville, TN: Holman Bible Publishers, 1991); and *PC Bible Atlas for Windows 1.0k*, Copyright 1993, Parsons Technology; components of "The QuickVerse Library, version 1.0g," copyright 1995, 1996 by Craig Rairdin and Parsons Technology, Inc., Hiawatha, IA.]
5. See 2 Tim. 3:8.
6. An article in *The Holman Bible Dictionary* titled "Pharaoh" notes that ancient pharaohs served as Egypt's absolute monarchs, military leaders, supreme judges and spiritual leaders. Pharaoh would demonstrate his "divine power" each morning by conducting "'the Rite of the House of the Morning,' an early morning ritual in which he broke the seal to the statue of the sun god [Amun-Re], waking him up with a prayer. This act brought the sun up and started every day for the people." Also see Exodus 7:14,15.
7. Henry H. Halley, *Halley's Bible Handbook: An Abbreviated Bible Commentary* (Grand Rapids, MI: Zondervan Publishing House, 1965), pp. 110, 111. Also see Exodus 14:20-22. Halley cites the claim by archaeologist Sir Flinders Petrie that each tribe in Egyptian society had its own god represented by an animal. The most notable are the three major gods of Egypt:

"*Ptah* (Apis), was god of Memphis, represented by a Bull. *Amon*, god of Thebes, was represented by a Cow . . . *Ra*, sun god, by a Hawk."

8. Ibid. Halley said Sir Petrie also noted that the Nile River was considered sacred and that the frog represented "Heka, a goddess." Also see Exod. 8:1-15.

9. See Exodus 8:16-19.

10. See Exodus 8:20-32.

11. See Exodus 9:1-7.

12. See Exodus 9:8-12.

13. See Exodus 9:13-32.

14. See Exodus 9:32. Egypt's wheat and spelt crops, unlike her flax and barley crops, were not destroyed by the hail because they bloomed later than other crops. The stalks were able to rebound from that pounding and come to maturity, just in time for the locusts to devour them. God does all things well, and that includes His ability to humble proud national leaders and nations.

15. All of the events I have described in this paragraph, with the exception of the events at the Cult of Osiris in Abydos, are found in Exodus 8:10-19. The fictitious events in Abydos and the other religious sites, temples and cities of Egypt were developed from archaeological evidence about them and from my interpretation of how their daily activities would have been disrupted by God's signs and wonders.

16. See Exodus 10:21-29.

17. This statement was extrapolated to demonstrate the meaning behind the actual sentiment in the Scriptures "We will all be dead" (Exod. 12:33).

18. See Exodus 13:18. The *King James Version* says the men were "harnessed," but newer translations make it clear this meant they marched "in martial array," or armed and ready for battle. As slaves, they had no weapons until Passover night.

19. See Exodus 11:7.

20. Exodus 14:2 records what God told Moses: "Tell the sons of Israel to turn back and camp before *Pi-hahiroth* [mouth of gorges], between *Migdol* [tower] and the sea; you shall camp in front of *Baal-zephon* [the god of destruction or god of winter cold], opposite it, by the sea." God purposely led His people into a trap but not to harm them. They were the bait for a pride-filled Pharaoh.

21. Exodus 14:25.

22. Derek Prince, *The Last Word on the Middle East* (Lincoln, VA: Chosen Books, 1982), p. 73.

Chapter 2

1. Lance Lambert, *The Uniqueness of Israel* (Eastbourne, England: Kingsway Publications Ltd., 1980), p. 55.

2. Ibid.

3. Merrill C. Tenney, *New Testament Survey* (Grand Rapids, MI: Wm. B. Eerdmans Publishing Co., 1961), p. 45. Lambert, *The Uniqueness of Israel*, p. 160, mentions Emperor Hadrian's attempt to rename Jerusalem and remove every trace of Jewish history from it.

4. Jim Goll, from an article titled, "Say to the North."

5. *Merriam Webster's Dictionary*, 10ᵗʰ Ed., s.v. "aliyah." The date, the Hebrew word and the definition may be found.

6. Kai Kjæ-Hansen, *Joseph Rabinowitz and the Messianic Movement: The Herzl of Jewish Christianity* (Grand Rapids, MI: Wm. B. Eerdmans Publishing Co.; and The Stables, Carberry, Scotland: The Handsel Press Ltd.; 1995), pp. 17, 18.

7. My narrative of Joseph Rabinowitz's supernatural revelation on the Mount of Olives has been reconstructed from several sources including transcripts of actual messages and the report of a student attending a meeting in Leipzig, Germany, on February 13, 1887, where Rabinowitz gave his testimony. According to author Kai Kjæ-Hansen, the details contained in this student's report "are probably the closest we can get to a description of Rabinowitz's 'conversion.'" Ibid., p. 19.

8. Ibid., p. 22.

9. Ibid., p. 33. I accompanied a prayer team to Kishinev in recent years.

10. Ibid.

11. Ibid.

12. Theodor Herzl, *The Jewish State*, trans. S. D'Avigdor, p. 15; quoted in Lance Lambert, *The Uniqueness of Israel*, p. 129, 130, emphasis mine.

13. Ibid., p. 79, emphasis mine.

14. Ibid., p. 130, emphasis mine.

15. Herzl, *Diary for September 3, 1897*; quoted in Tom Hess, Appendix B in *Let My People Go! The Struggle of the Jewish People to Return to Israel* (Washington, DC: Progressive Vision, 1988), p. 116; emphasis mine. (In November 1947, almost 50 years later, the United Nations General Assembly decided to recognize the right of the Jewish people to have their own state.)

16. Ramon Bennett, *SAGA: Israel and the Demise of Nations* (Jerusalem: Arm of Salvation, 1993), p. 149, 150. The specific application of acetone in the manufacture of cordite is briefly described in *Merriam Webster's Dictionary*, 10ᵗʰ Ed., s.v. "cordite."

17. Ibid., p. 150, emphasis mine.

18. Tom Hess, *Let My People Go!* p. 57.

19. Quoted in Ramon Bennett, *SAGA*, p. 150, emphasis mine.

20. Ramon Bennett, *When Day and Night Cease* (Jerusalem: Arm of Salvation Press, 1992), p. 92.

21. Jim W. Goll, *Kneeling on the Promises: Birthing God's Purposes Through Prophetic Intercession* (Grand Rapids, MI: Chosen Books, a division of Baker Book House Co., 1999), p. 195.

22. Steve Lightle, *Operation Exodus II* (Tulsa, OK: Insight Publishing, 1998), p. 154.

23. Ibid.

24. Ibid., p. 158.

25. Ulf Eckman, *The Jews: People of the Future* (Minneapolis, MN: Word of Life Publications, 1993), p. 70.

26. Gordon Lindsay, *The Miracle of Israel* (Dallas: Christ For The Nations, Inc., 1987), p. 46.

27. Ibid.

28. Ibid., p. 47.

29. Ibid., p. 51.

Chapter 3

1. Tom Hess, *The Watchmen: Being Prepared and Preparing the Way for Messiah* (Charlotte, NC: Morningstar Publications, 1998), p. 168; also Tom Hess, *Let My People Go!* (Washington, DC: Progressive Vision, 1988), p. 18.

2. John Hagee, *Final Dawn over Jerusalem* (Nashville, TN: Thomas Nelson Publishers, 1998): "I want you to see that church policy shaped the policy of the Third Reich. When Hitler signed the Concordant with the Roman Church, he said, 'I am only continuing the work of the Catholic Church.'" Then the author provides a shocking 16-point comparison of church policies and their tragic Nazi counterparts (pp. 58-60). I must mention that Hitler did not limit his admiration to the anti-Semitic leanings of the Roman Catholic Church—he was also a great admirer of Martin Luther, and particularly of the anti-Semitic writings characteristic of his later years.

3. Michael L. Brown, *Our Hands Are Stained with Blood* (Shippensburg, PA: Destiny Image Publishers, 1992), p. 91, citing Eliezer Berkovits, "Judaism in the Post-Christian Era," reprinted in Frank Ephraim Talmage, *Disputation and Dialogue: Readings in the Jewish-Christian Encounter* (New York: Ktav/Anti-Defamation League of B'nai B'rith, 1975), p. 287ff.

4. Ibid., pp. 10, 11; from quotes cited by Malcolm Hay, *The Roots of Christian Anti-Semitism* (New York: Liberty Press, 1981), p. 27.

5. Ibid.

6. Ibid., p. 11.

7. Dell F. Sanchez, *The Last Exodus* (San Antonio, TX: Jubilee Books, 1998), pp. 42, 43.

8. Ibid., p. 43.

9. Bernard Hamilton, *The Crusades* (Gloucestershire, UK: Sutton Publishing Limited, 1998), pp. 1, 2.

10. Ibid., p. 4.

11. Hagee, *Final Dawn over Jerusalem*, pp. 47, 48, citing Jonathan Riley-Smith, ed., *The Oxford Illustrated History of the Crusades* (New York: Oxford University Press, 1995), p. 81. According to Bernard Hamilton, *The Crusades*, p. 3, Pope Urban made it easy for knights and professional soldiers to defend the faith against Muslims in Jerusalem and Jews at home by fashioning a specialized crusade indulgence for them. This new quick version dispensed with the usual bread-and-water fasts and acts of public humiliation. All they had to do to get a papal indulgence for sins of violence was "make a solemn vow in the presence of a priest, confess their sins to him and wear a red cross on their cloaks."

12. Ibid., p. 48.

13. Brown, *Our Hands Are Stained with Blood*, p. 12; citing Edward H. Flannery, *The Anguish of the Jews: Twenty-Three Centuries of Anti-Semitism* (New York/Mahwah: Paulist Press, 1985), pp. 90, 91.

14. Ibid., pp. 13, 14; citing Malcolm Hay, *The Roots of Christian Anti-Semitism*, pp. 76, 81, 86-87.

15. Hagee, *Final Dawn over Jerusalem*, p. 50; citing Malcolm Hay, *The Roots of Christian Anti-Semitism* (USA: Anti-Defamation League of B'nai B'rith and Alice Ivy Hay, 1981), p. 37. Brown and Hagee each drew from the same work by Malcolm Hay, but evidently they used versions published under different publisher imprints.

16. Sanchez, *The Last Exodus*, p. 63.

17. Brown, *Our Hands Are Stained with Blood*, pp. 89, 90; citing Benjamin Shlomo Hamburger, *False Messiahs and Their Opposers* (Hebrew; B'nai Brak, Israel: Mechon Moreshet Ashkenaz, 1989), p. 19. The quotation at the end of the paragraph is from Rav Shimon Walbah, a leading Orthodox rabbi in Israel.

18. Sanchez, *The Last Exodus*, pp. 14, 15, with reference to Tarshish in 2 Chronicles 9:21 and 1 Kings 10:22.

19. *The Doubleday Dictionary for Home, School and Office*, s.v. "Sephardim."

20. Sanchez, *The Last Exodus*, p. 28.

21. Ibid., pp. 43-45.

22. Ibid., pp. 44-58.

23. Ibid., p. 59.

24. Hagee, *Final Dawn over Jerusalem*, p. 53.

25. Ibid.

26. Brown, *Our Hands are Stained with Blood*, n.p.

27. Sanchez, *The Last Exodus*, pp. 83-85.

28. Ulf Ekman, *The Jews—People of the Future* (Minneapolis, MN: Word of Life Publications, 1993—English edition), pp. 70, 71.

Chapter 4

1. The Commonwealth of Independent States (CIS) was formed in December 1991, after a tripartite agreement among Russia, Ukraine and Belarus created the nucleus of the new political center of the former USSR. It marked the end of Mikhail Gorbachev's political career as general secretary of the fallen Communist party and the temporary rise of former Moscow Communist party chief, Boris Yeltsin.
2. Microsoft Encarta Online Encyclopedia 2000, s.v. "Berlin Wall."
3. Steve Lightle, *Operation Exodus II* (Tulsa, OK: Insight Publishing, 1998), pp. 20, 21, 27-29; and Gustav Scheller with Jonathan Miles, *Operation Exodus* (Tonbridge, England: Sovereign World Limited, 1998; distributed in U.S. by Renew Books), pp. 29, 30.
4. Lightle, *Operation Exodus II*, pp. 45-47.
5. Scheller, *Operation Exodus,* pp. 73, 74.
6. Lightle, *Operation Exodus II*, pp. 55-59.
7. Tom Hess, *Let My People Go!* (Washington, DC: Progressive Vision, 1988), pp. 34-36.
8. Ibid., p. 36.
9. Ibid., pp. 36, 37.
10. Lightle, *Operation Exodus II*, p. 105.
11. Ibid., pp. 106, 107.
12. See "identificational repentance" in the glossary.
13. Deutsches Historisches Museum: Berlin. "A Concrete Curtain: The Life and Death of the Wall and Part 5: The Fall." http://www.wall-berlin.org/gb/chute_tex2.htm (accessed September 7, 2000).
14. Microsoft Encarta Online Encyclopedia 2000, s.v. "Berlin Wall."

Chapter 5

1. Steve Lightle with Eberhard Muehlan and Katie Fortune, *Exodus II: Let My People Go!* (Kingwood, TX: Hunter Books, 1983), pp. 66, 67.
2. Ibid., p. 229.
3. Gustav Scheller with Jonathan Miles, *Operation Exodus* (Tonbridge, England: Sovereign World Limited, 1998; distributed in U.S. by Renew Books), pp. 27, 28.
4. Ibid., pp. 28, 29.
5. Clyde Williamson with James Craig, *The Esther Fast Mandate: A Call to End-Time Intercession for the Release, Return, Restoration and Revival of Israel and the Church* (Etobicoke, Ontario: Almond Publications, 1987), p. 29.
6. Ibid., cover.
7. Tom Hess, *The Watchmen: Being Prepared and Preparing the Way for Messiah* (Charlotte, NC: MorningStar Publications, 1998), pp. 11, 12.

8. Mahesh and Bonnie Chavda, *Watch of the Lord: The Secret Weapon of the Last-Day Church* (Lake Mary, FL: Creation House, 1999), pp. 144, 145.

9. Ibid.

10. Ibid.

11. Ibid.

12. Michael Schiffmann, from a personal e-mail communication I received February 25, 2000.

Chapter 6

1. Gustav Scheller with Jonathan Miles, *Operation Exodus* (Tonbridge, England: Sovereign World Limited, 1998; distributed in U.S. by Renew Books), p. 43.

2. Ibid., pp. 46, 47.

3. Steve Lightle, *Operation Exodus II* (Tulsa, OK: Insight Publishing, 1998), p. 181.

4. Information cited from the September 2000 *Exobus Project Update*, the official newsletter of the Exobus Project, based in Hull, England. This ministry operates with a staff of volunteers from many different countries. For more information see appendix 5.

5. Sandra Teplinski, *Out of the Darkness: The Untold Story of Jewish Revival in the Former Soviet Union* (Jacksonville Beach, FL: HOIM Publishing, 1998), Foreword by Jonathan Bernis, p. xii.

6. Ibid., pp. xii, xiii.

7. In an interview, Jonathan Bernis said HOIM has held festivals in Moscow, Saint Petersburg, Nizhny Novgorad, Novosibersk and Kiev, Russia; Minsk, Belarus; Kishinev, Moldova; Riga, Latvia; Budapest, Hungary; and in Donesk, Vinnitsa, Zaparoshya, Nikaliev, Zhitomir and Odessa, Ukraine. He has also led festivals in India and Argentina. Fifteen Messianic-Jewish congregations in Eastern Europe have been founded or strengthened through the festivals. The largest congregation, located in Kiev, has about 800 members. For more information concerning Hear O Israel Ministries, visit the ministry's websites: HOIM.com or Jewishvoice.org.

8. Teplinski, *Out of the Darkness,* p. 80; citing Zvi Gitelman, "Soviet Reactions to the Holocaust, 1945-1991" in *The Holocaust in the Soviet Union,* Dobrozycki and Gurock, eds., p. 3. Teplinski, an attorney, wrote, "It is not widely known that approximately one third of the six million Jews killed in the Holocaust were living under Soviet rule at the onset of World War II."

9. The massacre at Babi Yar is well documented. Some notable sources for more detailed information include: Simon Wiesenthal Center, ed., *Babi Yar: 1941-1991* (Los Angeles: Simon Wiesenthal Center, 1991); and *Encyclopedia of the Holocaust,* (New York: MacMillan Publishing Co., 1990), vol. 1, s.v. "Babi Yar."

10. Kai Kjær-Hansen, *Joseph Rabinowitz and the Messianic Movement*, p. 68.

11. See Genesis 26:18-22.

12. Caleb was described as a man with "a different spirit" in Numbers 14:24. He is recognized as one of only two men in his generation with the ability to look past the enemies, obstacles, doubt and unbelief and clearly perceive the will and plan of God for His people.

13. See Revelation 16.

Chapter 7

1. Gail Harris, *The Gateway to Reconciliation: A True Story of the Love of God for His People the Jews As Told to Us by Pastor Helmuth and Uli Eiwen As They Lived It.* (Evergreen, CO: Evergreen Publications, 1997), p. 5.

2. Ibid.

3. Ibid., p. 15.

4. Ibid., p. 14.

5. This is the first of 12 segments in the public statement issued through the Generals of Intercession (GI) titled "A Word upon Entering the New Millennium: Apostolic Council of Prophetic Elders, November 30, 1999": "There will be a great harvest of Jews which will begin during this decade. This will particularly affect the Russian Jews around the world. There will be what some missiologists term a 'people movement' among them. There will also be a persecution of Jews in Russia that . . . will notably escalate during the fall of 2000. This is so serious that it requires an immediate response from the church in prayer. We believe that it is the devil's strategy to precipitate another holocaust, and that this prayer will help open a window of escape for those [who] feel called to leave, and a protection to those who are called to stay (Jer. 16:15,16)."

6. If you have questions or comments regarding this statement, please write to Generals of Intercession, P.O. Box 49788, Colorado Springs, CO 80949. The framers of this statement have observed the Jewish custom of omitting key letter(s) to honor the holy name of the Almighty by reproducing it only in part in written form.

Chapter 8

1. 2 Timothy 3:16.

2. Paul Yonggi Cho, *Daniel: Insight on the Life and Dreams of the Prophet from Babylon* (Lake Mary, FL: Creation House, 1990). Paul Yonggi Cho later changed his name to David Yonggi Cho.

3. Ibid., p. 144.

4. C. Peter Wagner, ed. and comp., *Engaging the Enemy: How to Fight and Defeat Territorial Spirits* (Ventura, CA: Regal Books, 1991).

5. I still keep a piece of the fallen Berlin Wall in my office as a memorial stone and heavenly treasure to remind me that if the walls came down once, then they can come down again.

6. Revelation 2:13, emphasis mine.

7. James Strong, "Greek Dictionary of the New Testament," *Strong's Exhaustive Concordance of the Bible* (Nashville, TN: Abingdon, 1890). "Pergamum," 4010, 4444, pp. 56, 63.

8. "Humann, Karl," *Encyclopaedia Britannica* http://www.eb.com (accessed January 16, 2001).

9. Paul Goble, "Russia: Analysis From Washington: Rise Of Anti-Semitism In Russia," (*Radio Free Europe / Radio Liberty*), July 28, 1999. http://www.-rferl.org/nca/features/1999/07/f.ru.990728125607.html (accessed January 16, 2001).

10. Rabbi David Levine, who lives in Budapest Hungary, e-mail message, February 6, 2000. A good background report on Joerg Haider can be found at the Anti-Defamation League's website: http:www.adl.org/back-grounders/joerg_haider.html.

11. Rick Stivers, e-mail message, June 22, 1999. Stivers had visited the B'nai Israel Synagogue in Sacramento. He wrote, "I just knelt and wept at the yellow crime scene tape that kept me ten feet away from the building, the water still flowing at my feet through the heaps of charred cinders all around me. I picked up a handful of the blackened remains and stuffed them in a paper lunch bag. I wanted to remember. My hands turned black, but it was OK. My elder brother's entire building was black; my hands would help me remember."

12. Abigail Zuger, "Russia Has Few Weapons As Infectious Diseases Surge," *New York Times.* http://archives.nytimes.com:80 (accessed January 15, 2001).

13. "Global Intelligence Update," *Stratfor, Inc.* http://www.stratfor.com/CIS/news/990805.htm (accessed March 23, 2000).

14. Michal Ann Goll recorded the dream in her diary and told me the details.

15. Chuck Pierce, from a personal e-mail communication.

16. "The Battle of Britain," *The Bible College of Wales, Swansea.* http://members.netscapeonline.co.uk/philaedwards/history.htm (accessed January 8, 2001). For more information about this unforgettable prayer journey to the Moravian Prayer Tower, read Jim Goll, *The Art of Intercession* (Shippensburg, PA: Revival Press, Destiny Image Publishers, 1997).

17. If you are serious about "effectual fervent prayer," then I encourage you to pick up copies of the following books: Norman Grubb, *Rees Howells: Intercessor* (Fort Washington, PA: Christian Literature Crusade, Cambridge, England: Lutterworth Press, 1952); and Doris M. Ruscoe, *The Intercession of Rees Howells* (Fort Washington, PA: Christian Literature Crusade, Cambridge, England: Lutterworth Press, 1988).

18. Gustav Scheller, *Operation Exodus: Prophecy Being Fulfilled* (Tonbridge, England: Sovereign World, 1998), appendix 2, pp. 150, 151.

Chapter 9

1. A full account of Evald Ruffy's story can be found in Jim Goll, *Kneeling on the Promises: Birthing God's Purposes Through Prophetic Intercession* (Grand Rapids, MI: Chosen Books, 1999).
2. Ephesians 2:19,20.
3. See Mark 16:20.
4. S. E. Gordon, *What Will It Take to Change the World?* (Grand Rapids, MI: Baker Book House, 1979), n.p.
5. See Matthew 10:16 and 1 Chronicles 12:32.
6. See Luke 18:1-8.

GLOSSARY OF TERMS

This brief glossary of terms may help clarify the meaning of certain words used in this book. By no means is it a thorough and comprehensive dictionary. Rather, I have simply defined these terms in my own words to be a blessing as you ponder the weighty issues in this book.

aliyah. The Hebrew word for the return of the Jews to their ancient covenant homeland in Israel. It literally means "going up." See "*Eretz Israel*" and "covenant."

angelic visitation. A time in which the heavenly ambassadors, or messengers, are released into the earthly realm and individuals experience their appearing. At times their presence can be felt, seen and heard. See "angels."

angels. These heavenly messengers are beings created by God for the primary purpose of worshiping Him. They also may go forth obeying the voice of His word (see Ps. 103:20,21) to declare the message of the Lord and to release displays of God's power, judgment and/or manifested presence. See "angelic visitation."

anointing. The presence and power of God manifested—or the manifested presence of God—working in, on or through an individual or corporate group, enabling them to do the works of Christ.

anti-Semitism/anti-Semitic. Intense dislike, hostility, hatred or discrimination against Jewish people, religious practices, culture or ethnicity.

Ashkenazi-Ashkenazim. A name which in its more popular use describes those Jewish people originating in northwest Europe, particularly Germany, Central Europe, Eastern Europe and Russia. It has become a designation of culture and way of life for Jewish people from those areas, as contrasted with the *Sephardi* culture.

awakening. A historic intervention of God's presence that revives the Church to such an extent that it affects society and brings it back into the moral values of God. North America has experienced two great awakenings, and some people believe the greatest awakening is about to be released on a worldwide level.

cessationism. A theological belief system stating that the gifts of the Holy Spirit ceased when the canon of Scripture was closed with the completion of the New Testament. Cessationists do not accept that the gifts of the Spirit are valid or necessary for today.

charismatic. Coming from the Greek word *charis* for "grace," this term was coined in the 1960s to describe those who believe that the gifts of the Holy Spirit are active today.

CIS. The CIS, or Commonwealth of Independent States, was formed in December 1991, after a tripartite agreement among Russia, Ukraine and Belarus created the nucleus of the new political center of the former USSR. It marked the end of Mikhail Gorbachev's political career as general secretary of the fallen Communist party and the temporary rise of former Moscow Communist party chief, Boris Yeltsin.

covenant. A solemn, binding agreement between two parties. The greatest of all covenants are those covenants God makes with individuals, nations and humankind. These eternal promises are as unshakeable and trustworthy as God Himself.

crisis intercession. Petitioning the Father intensely for His mercy to be extended in the midst of prevailing circumstances or for His judgment to be withheld. A central focus of this book is God's mandate upon the Church to enter intensive *crisis intervention* on behalf of the Jewish people still dwelling in the Land of the North and in other lands outside Israel.

Day of Atonement. The most holy day for the Jews, an annual day of fasting, penitence and sacrifice for sin. Before the destruction of the Temple, the high priest would enter the Holy of Holies on the 10th day of the seventh month of the Hebrew calendar and offer sacrifices for the sanctuary, the priests and the people. This foreshadowed the entrance of Jesus, the great high priest, who offered Himself as our eternal sacrifice once for all, having purchased for us eternal salvation. This day, also known as Yom Kippur, is observed today with fasting and confession of sins.

deliverance. A Holy Spirit encounter by which an individual is set free in the name of Jesus from the oppression of evil spirits and also from circumstances that oppress from without.

demonization. The state of being under the influence or control of a demonic power.

diaspora. A dispersion of a people from their homeland, such as the Jewish people being sent into Egypt in the time of Moses or their desperate flight from Jerusalem and Israel in the latter years of the Roman Empire—in fulfillment of the prophecy of Jesus Christ.

dream. The inspired pictures and impressions given to the heart while one is sleeping. These are given by the Holy Spirit in order to teach, exhort, reveal, warn, cleanse or heal.

encounter. A personal experience in which an individual or group is confronted with the living reality of the Lord Jesus Christ by the present-day work of the Holy Spirit.

Eretz Israel. This Hebrew term means "the land of Israel."

evangelicals. Christians who zealously believe in the inerrancy of Scripture and the classic doctrines of the Church—including the deity of Jesus Christ, His atoning death and His bodily ascension and return.

fishers. (See "hunters and fishers.")

forerunner. One who goes before, so as to prepare the way for another. This term is commonly used today to describe the prophetic (such as John the Baptist) preceding the apostolic (such as Jesus Christ).

Fruit of the Spirit. A reference to Galatians 5:22,23 concerning love, joy, peace, patience, kindness, goodness, faithfulness, gentleness and self-control. These are the qualities of a person's life that comprise his or her godly character.

gatekeepers. The elders of a city or church who have the authority to open or close the gates of a city as alerted by the watchmen.

Gentile. This Hebrew word literally means "nation," but it is used to describe any person who is neither of Jewish origin nor an adherent of Judaism. (See "righteous Gentile.")

gift of discerning of spirits. Supernatural perception given by God to enable believers to distinguish the motivating spirit behind words or deeds, and to discern the source of operation as human, demonic or of the Holy Spirit.

gift of prophecy. The supernatural ability to hear the voice of the Holy Spirit and speak God's mind or counsel. Given for the purposes of edifying, exhorting, comforting, convicting, instructing, imparting and testifying of and from Jesus.

gift of tongues. The supernatural ability given by God to enable believers to speak in a language, whether earthly or heavenly, that they have not learned in the natural realm. This gift is used in prayer, communion with God, to edify the one speaking, as well as to supernaturally communicate a message in a language known by those listening.

gifts of the Spirit. The expression of God's power at work, given by the Holy Spirit, to be used at special times for special occasions. Such gifts as recorded in 1 Corinthians 12:4-11 attest to the empowering of the Holy Spirit and are vital in the "signs and wonders" ministry.

Hasid-Hasidism (also Chasid-Chasidism). A popular religious movement within Judaism which began in the latter part of the eighteenth century. At first it was bitterly contested by orthodoxy, but it was finally accepted and recognized. It was characterized by religious ecstasy, mass enthusiasm, a close-knit and cohesive community life and charismatic personalities in leadership.

healing evangelist. A person who heralds the Gospel and is accompanied by signs, wonders, miracles and healing.

Holocaust. The word is derived from Greek and means "a whole burnt offering; wholesale sacrifice to destruction." It is the name given to the most tragic period of the second Jewish exile. It spans a period of 12 years, from 1933 to 1945. The last six years of this period, 1939-45, were the worst. It was the Nazi-inspired "final solution" to the so-called Jewish problem, and it called for the systematic liquidation of the Jewish people. It is conservatively estimated that as least 6 million Jews died in this period.

hunters and fishers. "Behold, I am going to send for many *fishermen*," declares the LORD, "and they will fish for them; and afterwards I will send for *many hunters*, and they will hunt them from every mountain and every hill and from the clefts of the rocks" (Jer. 16:16, emphasis mine). Fishermen are benevolent messengers sent to the Jewish people to encourage, woo and entice them to obey God's call to flee foreign lands and return to Israel. They are benevolent because they wish only good upon the Jewish people. Their mission is to extend mercy and deliverance to a divine destiny and from impending danger. Hunters, on the other hand, operate under the influence of the spirit of Haman or some other satanic force, to hunt down and round up every Jewish person they can find with only one ultimate goal—absolute annihilation of the Jewish people.

identificational repentance. In essence, it involves the powerful and solemn ministry of identifying with our historical roots in intercession and repentance, which releases both freedom from yesterday's sins and an outpouring of God's promises and prophetic blessings. It is based on the truth that individual and corporate sin can only be removed through biblical confession and repentance before God. Identificational repentance is a biblical practice revealed in the lives and ministry of Daniel, Ezra, Esther, Moses and even Jesus Christ our Lord. More than any other, He identified with our sin (although He had committed no sin), took it upon Himself and "repented" to the Father for it on our behalf. Identificational repentance is the central subject of Jim Goll's book, *Father Forgive Us! Freedom from Yesterday's Sin* (Shippensburg, PA: Destiny Image Publishers, 1999).

intercession. The act of making a request to a superior, or expressing a deep-seated yearning to our one and only superior, God.

intercessor. One who reminds God of His promises and appointments yet to be fulfilled; who takes up a case of injustice before God on behalf of another; who makes up the "hedge" (that is, builds up the wall in time of battle); and who stands in the gap between God's righteous judgments and the people's need for mercy.

laying on of hands. A method of ministering to individuals for consecration, ordination, gift impartation, healing and blessing. This was a practice in Old and New Testament times and in the Early Church. It was restored to the Body of Christ in the last century as an accepted model.

manifested presence of God. While God is omnipresent, or everywhere, He nevertheless reveals or manifests His presence strategically and locationally.

neo-Nazi. This term describes new Nazis: those today who agree with or follow the programs and principles of Hitler's Nazi party, particularly his extreme anti-Semitism.

Olim. Those "going up" to Israel from other lands.

open vision. A kind of vision in which the natural eyes are open and the believer is seeing and perceiving realities in the spiritual world.

paradigm. A model or pattern of thought seen in society. The term "paradigm shift" is commonly used to describe trends or developments that are creating a new way of viewing things.

Pentecostal. A Christian who emphasizes the baptism in the Holy Spirit with the accompanying gift of speaking in tongues, generally connected with several Pentecostal denominations.

pogrom. This Russian word meaning "destruction," or "devastation," describes the organized or officially encouraged slaughter of Jewish people through militia-led riots in Russia, the Ukraine, Poland, Romania and parts of Eastern Europe (particularly during the time of the Russian tsars).

presbytery. A group of elders or leaders in the church; overseers set to watch over and care for the congregation.

priest. One who pleads the needs of the people before God. In the Old Testament a special tribe, the Levites, was set apart for this purpose. In the New Testament each believer in Christ is a priest unto the Lord.

priestly intercession. An intercessory task in which the priest not only represents himself before the Lord but, like priests of old, carries the 12 stones of Israel on his heart—the burdens, needs and cares of others— before the great High Priest.

prophet/prophetess. A man or woman who represents the interests of God to the people. Having stood in the council of God, the prophet releases a clarion call to the people of what is in God's heart at the moment. Some refer to this as one of the fivefold ministry gifts listed in Ephesians 4:11.

prophetic destiny. The revelatory promise of God portraying His purposes, plans and pursuits for an individual, group, city or nation.

prophetic intercession. The act of waiting before God in order to hear or receive His burden—His word, concern, warning, condition, vision or promise—and responding back to Him and the people with appropriate actions.

prophetic presbytery. A selected group of seasoned, mature revelatory gifted believers ministering together over individuals and or congregations often with the laying on of hands.

prophetic priests. Individuals who hold the Old Testament offices of prophet and priest with New Testament applications for today. They not only hear from the Lord the pronouncements from His throne but pray the promises back to the Father.

prophetic unction/anointing. This occurs when one is impressed by the Holy Spirit to speak, sing or act out what has been revealed by the special enduement of grace.

radical. Basic change that alters society. Someone who is seeking to change the current status of the Church, calling it back to its original roots.

refuseniks. These primarily Jewish residents of the former USSR received worldwide coverage when they chose to risk their lives to protest the bureaucratic denial of their applications for immigration. Russian Jews knew that simply by applying to leave the USSR for Israel they would probably lose their jobs, be denied basic privileges, endure harassment from the secret police and local Communist party officials, and possibly face prison time.

renewal. To make something new that has been growing stale. This is a term used in relation to movements within the Church, such as "charismatic renewal." See "charismatic."

repentance. A turning around to go in the opposite direction—making a 180-degree turn. A change of heart that alters outward behavior. A turning away from sin and turning toward the Lord and His ways.

replacement theology. The theological teaching that God is through with the Jewish people, and that the Church has replaced Israel in the plan and purpose of God. According to this view, God's promised blessings to Israel in the Hebrew Scriptures are now the *exclusive* property of the Church, because God has cursed and rejected Israel. The Church is seen as the new or true Israel because of the role the Jewish people played in the rejection and crucifixion of Jesus the Messiah. However, it is clear that Jew and Gentile worked together to crucify the Savior of the world and that He died to bring forgiveness and new life to both through His own death and resurrection.

restoration. To recover or return to an original state or condition. The progressive pattern of recalling a person, church or community to its former place of influence and impact (see Acts 3:19-21).

revival. To revive something, to bring it back to life. In Church history, it is a term used to call the Church back to a place of vigor and life and to renew her call to evangelism and to be salt and light in the world.

revolution. A sudden shift or change in society that affects history—as a call to return to radical authentic Christianity.

righteous Gentile. The government of Israel uses this term to officially honor those non-Jews who risked their lives, freedom, safety, reputation and livelihood to save, protect, shield or assist Jewish people from their pursuers during World War II and at other times.

Sephardi-Sephardim. A name which, in its strictly correct use, refers only to those Jews of Spanish or Portuguese origin (*Sepharad* means "Spain" in Hebrew). In its popular use, however, it has a far wider meaning, designating all Latin Jews and those from the Mediterranean region. It is also used to describe the Jewish culture and way of life which originated in this area.

spirit of revelation. The unfolding or unveiling of God's will to the eyes of the heart. The revelation of truth otherwise unknown can come through impressions, prophecy, dreams, visions and messages from the Lord.

spiritual warfare. The confrontation of the kingdom of darkness by the power of the kingdom of God in order to displace the works of darkness and elevate His Son, Jesus.

supplication. To entreat, seek, implore or beseech God in earnest prayer.

Talmud. This Hebrew word means "study," or "learning." It is used most commonly to describe that body of teaching which comprises the commentary and discussions of scholars. Composed between A.D. 200 and A.D. 400, it consists of two parts:

- The *Mishnah*, which is the collection of the oral laws or traditions of the elders, as opposed to the written law of God, was compiled and edited by Rabbi Judah Ha-Nasi (A.D. 230). Its object was to preserve the law of God and to apply it to everyday life. From the time of its compilation by Rabbi Judah, in Jewish eyes it has ranked second only to the Old Testament. The word "mishnah" comes from a root meaning "to repeat" and thus "to teach by repetition."
- The *Gemara* is the record of the commentary and discussion on the Mishnah. "Gemara" means "completion" or "tradition." There are two Gemaras, one compiled in Tiberias by Rabbi Johanan in the fourth century A.D. and the other compiled in Babylon towards the end of the fifth century A.D. Thus the Mishnah with the Tiberias Gemara is popularly called "The Jerusalem Talmud," and the Mishnah with the Babylonian Gemara is called "The Babylonian Talmud." The influence of the Talmud upon Jewish life, thought and conduct is inestimable.

travail. An intense form of prayer that brings forth a birthing in the spirit, which creates or enlarges an opening for an increased dimension of the kingdom of God.

vision. Sight disclosed supernaturally to the spiritual eyes. There are various levels of visions—eyes open, eyes closed, panoramic (moving) and still frame shots.

visionary revelation. The grace of the Holy Spirit that enables a Christian to experience such manifestations as visions and dreams.

visitation. A supernatural experience in which a distinct sense of the presence of God is accompanied by fear of the Lord. This may come in the form of an angelic visitation, as in the book of Acts, or by other biblical means.

waiting. A posture of stillness before the Lord when the person is being attentive to the moving of His Spirit.

watch of the Lord. A gathering in Jesus' name (see Matt. 24; Mark 13; Luke 21) to watch, pray and be vigilant for the life of a church, city or nation. It is also a position on the wall of the Lord in order to see outside the city, in order to alert the gatekeepers to approaching enemies or envoys from the King; and inside the city to recognize and confront disorderly, unlawful activity of the enemy within.

watchmen. Those who serve in the position of watching. See "watch of the Lord."

word of knowledge. Supernatural revelation by the Holy Spirit that discloses the truth or fact He wishes to make known about a person or situation.

word of wisdom. Supernatural revelation by the Holy Spirit that discloses the remedy, solution or way of God that He wishes to make known for that particular situation.

worship. Posturing our hearts in awe and reverence before God, bowing down before Him. We worship God for who He is and we praise Him for what He has done.

Zionism. The movement birthed and organized by Theodor Herzl, who believed the true destiny of the Jewish people could only be found in a national home of their own, in Zion, their ancient covenant home. These "lovers of Zion" urged the Jewish people to flee Europe and return to their ancient homeland for decades before Hitler's storm troopers began to herd millions of European Jews to their destruction.

RECOMMENDED READING

Accattoli, Luigi. *When a Pope Asks Forgiveness: The Mea Culpas of John Paul II.* Boston, MA: Pauline Books & Media, 1998.

Archbold, Norma. *The Mountains of Israel.* N.p.: Phoebe's Song Publications, 1993.

Bennett, Ramon. *Saga: Israel and the Demise of Nations.* Jerusalem: Arm of Salvation Press, 1993.

——. *When Day and Night Cease: A Prophetic Study of World Events and How Prophecy Concerning Israel Affects the Nations, the Church and You.* Jerusalem: Arm of Salvation Press, 1992.

Brown, Michael L. *Our Hands Are Stained with Blood: The Tragic Story of the "Church" and the Jewish People.* Shippensburg, PA: Destiny Image Books, 1997.

Buss, Gerald. *Bear's Hug: Christian Belief and the Soviet State, 1917-1986.* Grand Rapids, MI: Wm. B. Eerdmans Publishing Co., 1987.

Chapman, Matthew. *Spiritual Geography.* Waco, TX: n.p., 1992.

Chavda, Mahesh and Bonnie. *Watch of the Lord: The Secret Weapon of the Last-Day Church.* Lake Mary, FL: Creation House, Strang Communications Company, 1999.

Cho, Paul Yonggi. *Daniel: Insight on the Life and Dreams of the Prophet from Babylon.* Lake Mary, FL: Creation House, Strang Communications Company, 1990.

Ekman, Ulf. *The Jews: People of the Future.* Minneapolis, MN: Word of Life Publications, 1993.

Facius, Johannes. *As in the Days of Noah: God's Judgment on the Nations.* Tonbridge, England: Sovereign World, 1997.

Finto, Don. *Your People Shall Be My People.* Ventura, CA: Regal Books, 2001.

Goll, Jim W. *Father Forgive Us! Finding Freedom from the Sins of the Past.* Shippensburg, PA: Destiny Image Publishers, Inc., 1999.

——. *Kneeling on the Promises: Birthing God's Purposes Through Prophetic Intercession.* Grand Rapids, MI: Chosen Books, 1999.

——. *The Lost Art of Intercession.* Shippensburg, PA: Destiny Image Publishers, Inc., Revival Press, 1997.

Goll, Jim W. and Michal Ann Goll. *Encounters with a Supernatural God.* Shippensburg, PA: Destiny Image Publishers, Inc., 1998.

Goll, Michal Ann. *Women on the Frontlines.* Shippensburg, PA: Destiny Image Publishers Inc., 1999.

Grubb, Norman. *Rees Howells, Intercessor.* Fort Washington, PA: Christian Literature Crusade, 1987.

Hagee, John. *Final Dawn over Jerusalem.* Nashville, TN: Thomas Nelson Publishers, 1998.

Hess, Tom. *Let My People Go! The Struggle of the Jewish People to Return to Israel*, 2nd ed. Washington, DC: Progressive Vision, 1988.

——. *The Watchmen: Being Prepared and Preparing the Way for Messiah*. Charlotte, NC: MorningStar Publications, 1998.

Hamilton, Bernard. *The Crusades*. Phoenix Mill, Gloucester, England: Sutton Publishing, Ltd., 1998.

Harris, Gail. *The Gateway to Reconciliation: A True Story of the Love of God for His People the Jews as Told to Us by Pastor Helmuth and Uli Eiwen As They Lived It*. Evergreen, CO: Golden Eagle Publications, 1997.

Josephus. *Josephus: The Jewish War*, ed. G. A. Williamson. New York: Penguin Books, 1970.

Juster, Dan. *Jewish Roots: A Foundation of Biblical Theology*. Shippensburg, PA: Destiny Image Publishers, Inc., 1995.

Kjær-Hansen, Kai. *Joseph Rabinowitz and the Messianic Movement: The Herzl of Jewish Christianity*. Grand Rapids, MI: Wm. B. Eerdmans Publishing Co. and The Stables, Carberry, Scotland: The Handsel Press Ltd.; 1995.

LaHaye, Tim F. *The Coming Peace in the Middle East*. Grand Rapids, MI: Zondervan Publishing House, 1984.

Lambert, Lance. *Battle for Israel*. Eastbourne, England: Kingsway Publications, 1976.

——. *The Uniqueness of Israel*. Eastbourne, England: Kingsway Publications, Ltd., 1991.

Lightle, Steve. *Exodus II: Let My People Go!* Kingwood, TX: Hunter Books, 1983.

——. *Operation Exodus II: Answers You Need to Know About Explosive Future Events*. Tulsa, OK: Insight Publishing Group, 1998.

Lindsay, Gordon. *The Miracle of Israel*. Dallas: Christ For The Nations, Inc., 1987.

Lindsey, Hal. *The Late Great Planet Earth*. Grand Rapids, MI: Zondervan Publishing House, 1970.

Miller, Danny. *God, Israel, the Future and You*. Platteville, CO: Shalom Publications, 1988.

Prince, Derek. *Our Debt to Israel*. Fort Lauderdale, FL: Derek Prince Publications, 1977.

——. *Prophetic Destinies: Who Is Israel? Who Is the Church?* Lake Mary, FL: Creation House, Strang Communications Company, 1992.

——. *The Destiny of Israel and the Church: Restoration and Redemption at the End of the Age*. Milton Keynes, England: Word (UK) Ltd., 1992.

——. *The Last Word on the Middle East*. Lincoln, VA: Chosen Books, 1982.

Prince, Lydia. *Appointment in Jerusalem: As Told to Her Husband, Derek Prince*. Chappaqua, NY: Chosen Books, 1975, distributed by F. H. Revell Company.

Ruscoe, Doris M. *The Intercession of Rees Howells*. Fort Washington, PA: Christian Literature Crusade, 1988.

Sanchez, Dell F. *The Last Exodus*. San Antonio, TX: Jubilee Books, 1998.

Scheller, Gustav. *Operation Exodus: Prophecy Being Fulfilled.* Tonbridge, England: Sovereign World, 1998.

Schroeter, Leonard. *The Last Exodus.* Seattle, WA: University of Washington Press, 1974.

Sjöberg, Kjell. *The Prophetic Church.* Chichester, England: New Wine Press, 1992.

Ten Boom, Corrie. *The Hiding Place.* Uhlrichsville, Ohio: Barbour & Company, 2000.

Teplinski, Sandra. *Out of the Darkness: The Untold Story of Jewish Revival in the Former Soviet Union.* Jacksonville Beach, FL: HOIM Publishing, 1998.

Wagner, C. Peter, ed. *Engaging the Enemy: How to Fight and Defeat Territorial Spirits.* Ventura, CA: Regal Books, 1991.

Walvoord, John F. *The Nations in Prophecy.* Grand Rapids, MI: Zondervan Publishing House, 1967.

Williamson, Clyde and James Craig, *The Esther Fast Mandate: A Call to End-Time Intercession for the Release, Return, Restoration and Revival of Israel and the Church.* Etobicoke, Ontario: Almond Publications, 1987.

RECOMMENDED AUDIOTAPE/CD

Goll, Jim W. *Prayers for Israel with Jim W. Goll.* Kelowna, British Columbia: RevivalNow! Resources, 1999. This audiotape may be ordered online at www.jimgoll.com.

About the Author

Jim Goll and his wife, Michal Ann, are cofounders of Ministry to the Nations, based in Franklin, Tennessee, dedicated to releasing God's presence through the prophetic and intercessory activity emphasizing equipping and missions endeavors.

After pastoring for 13 years in the Midwest, Jim was thrust into the role of itinerant teaching and training. He has a heart to lift up the hands of leaders around the world. Jim's passion is to see a great revolution transpire in the Body of Christ and for the Church to become the house of prayer for all nations that Jesus declared that we would be. He has traveled extensively across North, South and Central America, Europe and Asia. He is the author of 8 books and 13 training manuals. He is currently an instructor in the Wagner Leadership Institute and the Christian Leadership University. He also founded Heart of David Ministry Institute. He is a member of the Apostolic Council of Prophetic Elders and the Caleb Company; a prophetic and prayer advisor to regional, national and international ministries and councils; and a contributing writer for several periodicals.

Jim and Michal Ann have been married for 25 years. They have four wonderful children and reside in the beautiful hills of Franklin, Tennessee.

FOR MORE INFORMATION:

JIM W. GOLL
MINISTRY TO THE NATIONS
P.O. BOX 1653
FRANKLIN, TN 37065
OFFICE PHONE: 615-599-5552
OFFICE FAX: 615-599-5554

E-mail: MTTN@earthlink.net, or
info@ministrytothenations.org

Website access: www.mttnweb.com, or
www.ministrytothenations.org, or
www.jimgoll.com

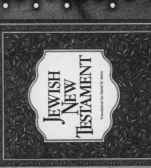

More Inspirational Reading

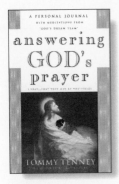

Answering God's Prayer
A Personal Journal with
Meditations from *God's
Dream Team*
Tommy Tenney
Paperback
ISBN 08307.25784

Go and Sin No More
A Call to Holiness
Michael L. Brown
Paperback
ISBN 08307.23897

God's Dream Team
A Call to Unity
Tommy Tenney
Paperback
ISBN 08307.23846

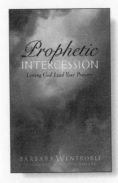

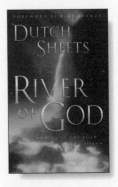

**Knockin' at
Heaven's Door**
God's Spirit Can Touch
Your Life
Stephen Hill
Paperback
ISBN 08307.24931

Prophetic Intercession
Unlocking Miracles and
Releasing the Blessings
of God
Barbara Wentroble
Paperback
ISBN 08307.23765

The River of God
Moving in the Flow of
God's Plan for Revival
Dutch Sheets
Paperback
ISBN 08307.20758

Regal
FROM GOSPEL LIGHT